The
10 Laws
of
Enduring
Success

Also by Maria Bartiromo

USE THE NEWS

*How to Separate the Noise from the Investment Nuggets
and Make Money in Any Economy*

The
10 Laws
of
Enduring
Success

Maria
Bartiromo

with Catherine Whitney

CROWN
BUSINESS
NEW YORK

CROWN BUSINESS is a trademark and CROWN and the Rising Sun
colophon are registered trademarks of Random House, Inc.

Originally published in hardcover in the United States by
Crown Business, an imprint of the Crown Publishing Group,
a division of Random House, Inc., New York, in 2010.

Library of Congress Cataloging-in-Publication Data
Bartiromo, Maria.
The 10 laws of enduring success / Maria Bartiromo
with Catherine Whitney.
p.   cm.
Includes index.
1. Success in business. 2. Success. 3. Self-actualization
(Psychology). I. Whitney, Catherine. II. Title.
III. Title: Ten laws of enduring success.
HF5386.B2717   2010
650.1—dc22   2009042267

ISBN 978-0-307-45253-5
eISBN 978-0-307-45254-2

BOOK DESIGN BY BARBARA STURMAN
JACKET PHOTOGRAPH BY MONICA RICH KOSANN

First Paperback Edition

146122990

To my grandfather,

CARMINE BARTIROMO,

who brought his dreams to America on the Rex *in 1919
and made my future success possible*

Contents

Prologue

Born on September 11

Redefining success

I was born on September 11, 1967, and always enjoyed the dramatic signature of my birth date: 911. I got a lot of mileage out of it over the years, calling friends and saying, "This is an emergency. Come to a birthday party." But that all changed with the *real* September 11, the one the world will never forget, on the day I turned thirty-four.

I arrived early for work at the New York Stock Exchange, where I was doing hourly market reports for CNBC, to find a big bouquet of flowers on my desk and a happy birthday message from my editorial assistant. It was a glorious morning in New York City, although the bright skies were hidden from view in the Exchange's windowless world. I was sitting in my tiny office above the trading floor when the news flashed on the screen that a plane had hit the World Trade Center, two blocks away. My boss at CNBC headquarters in New Jersey called and said, "Go outside and report to us what's happening," and in a flash I was up and running, down to the corner of Broadway and Wall Street. The Twin Towers were two blocks away, and a heavy cloud of smoke was billowing from one of them, causing people to stop and gape upward. I joined the crowd and started reporting what I was seeing, completely in the moment, my instincts sharp.

As I stood there watching and talking into my cell phone, the shadow of another plane appeared briefly overhead, and then that plane slammed into the World Trade Center's second tower. Like everyone else, I could not believe what I was witnessing. A great cry went up from the crowd, and a man standing next to me said softly, "The world has changed." I swung around to look at him. "What do you mean?" I asked, but I already knew the answer by the time he responded: "This is not an accident. It's terrorism."

I remained outside, calling in to report what I was seeing, as the smoke billowed from the buildings. I was still standing on the corner of Broadway and Wall when the first tower collapsed and everything around me turned black. Choking on smoke and buffeted by a raging wind of debris, I shielded my eyes and ran for my life. I didn't want to go back into the Exchange because I feared it could be another target, so I ducked into the stairwell of a building across the street, down three steps into a foyer where a small group of people were huddled. One woman was crying hysterically, and I remember thinking that this was not the time for panic or tears, that we had to keep our heads. I went over to her and said loudly and firmly,

"Please calm down. It's important that you calm down." And she did, even as the floor we were standing on began to shake with the force of the second tower collapsing. For the first time in my thirty-four years, I understood that I was in a life-and-death crisis, unsure whether I would survive.

We stayed that way for what seemed like hours but was only about twenty minutes, until the thunderous noise stopped and left everything eerily silent. I walked up onto the street, covered in soot, and I noticed that my black patent-leather shoes were white with a thick dust. There was debris from the collapsed buildings littering the ground, and thousands of scraps of burned papers flying around me. I stumbled across the street to the Stock Exchange, where the doors were shut tight. Eric, the NYSE security guard, peered out at me from the window and hurriedly opened a door. He stared at me as if he were seeing a ghost. "Maria," he cried, "what are you doing out here?" He grabbed my arm and pulled me inside.

The Exchange was crowded, but some people were joining a line of people forming on the eastern edge of Manhattan to walk uptown and away from the tragedy. I cleaned myself up as well as I could and went on the air—and stayed there reporting for the rest of the day from inside the NYSE. No one knew what would happen or when the Stock Exchange would reopen. We were all incredibly sobered to be right there in the business capital of the world, now Ground Zero, feeling as if our foundations were crumbling around us. I didn't want to imagine the terrible carnage just two blocks away.

I left the Exchange around 9:00 p.m., accompanied by my colleague Bob Pisani, who had been reporting alongside me throughout the day. The entire area was lit up with the recovery efforts. We walked nearly two miles up to 14th Street, where we were able to get a subway. The train was crowded, but nearly silent. The whole city was in a state of shock. As I arrived home and opened the door, I suddenly remembered that it was my birthday. When I walked in, my husband came over and we hugged wordlessly. He knew I was safe, because he'd been watching me on television, but it was an emotional moment.

When the Stock Exchange reopened on September 17, we were all facing the new normal. Wall Street was ugly, with a putrid smell that clung to our clothes and made it hard to breathe. For days I never stepped outside without putting on the white mask that the police provided for workers in the area. Many people were talking about wanting to move out of New York City. Still, when the Stock Exchange reopened that morning, it was an incredibly proud moment. Governor George Pataki, Mayor Rudy Giuliani, NYSE CEO Dick Grasso, and a group of firefighters rang the opening bell as the packed floor cheered. The world was watching as we stood tall against disaster. We had survived.

In the weeks and months to come, I had the opportunity to interview many people about 9/11, and as I did so,

I kept thinking, "This is the heart and soul of our country." It was a terrible blow that shattered our national self-image, but ultimately, as we rose from the fire and ashes, we showed the world what we were really made of.

Many people from all walks of life died on September 11. But because my job involved reporting on business and finance, it was the young stockbrokers I couldn't get out of my mind—the promising lives that had been stolen in the attacks. All of those men and women, who had done everything right and were so successful, with their great careers and nice homes and beautiful families. They were rising stars at places like Cantor Fitzgerald, a firm that lost six hundred and fifty-eight employees in the attacks. Their success had brought them to jobs at the World Trade Center, where their lives were snuffed out. It struck me that you could do everything perfectly in life, and still something could happen that would take it all away in an instant.

After 9/11 we experienced a national moment of truth—a time for reexamining what really mattered. Life not only throws curves, it can make you a victim of random terror or destruction. How can you be the one left standing? It was a time to reflect about what's important and what is not. Many, myself included, started thinking about how to persevere in difficult times. That reflection brought me back to my foundation. I am blessed with having the kind of roots that are deep and strong, with receiving the best kind of grounding possible as I grew up.

My father, Vincent Bartiromo, was a first-generation American, and my mother, Josephine, was second-generation, so I was raised with that indomitable immigrant work ethic. We lived in Bay Ridge, Brooklyn, a working-class neighborhood with a large Italian population, many of them the children and grandchildren of immigrants. My father owned a restaurant called the Rex Manor, which he'd inherited from his father, Carmine Bartiromo. It was named after the *Rex*, the great Italian ocean liner that brought my grandfather to America in 1919. I recently found pictures of the ship, along with the ship's manifest and a copy of my grandfather's green card. I felt so much pride, imagining what it was like for my grandfather and his fellow travelers. They left behind family and homes they loved and chose to head to America, based on a dream. The promise of freedom and opportunity was that powerful. And once they arrived, they never stopped striving. What courage my grandfather had—first to fight for his country, Italy, in World War I and then to leave his homeland and board a ship headed to Ellis Island to start a new life. I can only imagine what it must have taken for him to build his restaurant, proudly named after the ship that brought him here, providing his family, myself included, such opportunity.

Dad inherited my grandfather's work ethic. Work was life. From a very young age I was taught that there were no shortcuts. If you wanted to live the American dream, you had to work for it.

In all of my memories of childhood, whenever I picture my dad, he is standing in a corner of the Rex Manor kitchen, cooking and sweating profusely, with a bandanna tied around his head. The Rex Manor was a large and bustling place, part restaurant and part catering hall. Weekend wedding receptions, anniversaries, baptisms, and bar mitzvahs brought big crowds. The main catering hall could seat four hundred, and a smaller hall two hundred. Dad was always working. If I needed to talk to him, I could find him there in the same spot, literally laboring over a hot stove.

My memories of my mom also involve work. She had a full-time job at Off-Track Betting, where she was a teller toiling in the smoke-filled rooms, crowded primarily with men placing bets on the horses. My mom loved her job, mostly because it gave her financial independence. I still remember the lessons she taught me about this, and how she saved the money she made. She also loved her job because the atmosphere of the races was exciting, although she was not a gambler. Her job enabled her to send us to the best schools, to create extra treats for us, and to help support the family. Her first job in life, of course, was raising a family, which she did so well. Her sweat and tears are the reason I was able to prosper and learn the value of hard work and courage. I can still picture her coming home from work, walking down the street, juggling seven bags of groceries. She never stopped. She remains my hero.

In my family, the work ethic was something that got passed down from generation to generation, like a precious inheritance. So, when I was a teenager, I had a job after school and on weekends as a coat-check girl at Dad's restaurant. It was fun for me, because not only was it a job, but I was surrounded by family—and the tips were great, especially when there was a wedding. The charge was fifty cents, and most guests gave me a dollar. I enjoyed being able to earn money for myself. Later, when I was in college, I got a job at the OTB on Saturdays, and if you don't mind being in a smoke-filled room, it was a pretty great deal, with a higher salary than they were paying at fast-food restaurants. Knowing that you have to earn your own way is great preparation for handling those inevitable curveballs.

It would never have occurred to my parents to gripe about how hard they worked, to think that their lives were tougher than other people's, or to feel entitled to have more for less effort. Even today, if I complain about being overworked, my mother rolls her eyes and says, "Come on, Maria, you're not chopping trees."

I have to laugh—no sympathy there! "You're right, Mom. I'm not chopping trees."

It's true. I know how lucky I am, because I'm doing work I love, in the greatest place in the world, during the most exciting time in history. Wall Street really is the center of the universe—the place where the hopes and dreams of millions come together along narrow streets that remind us of the early days of our nation. And I have a front-row seat. I am a witness to a critical moment, when the very foundations of capitalism are being challenged. My twenty years on Wall Street have been something of a roller-coaster ride of highs and lows: the greatest bull market ever seen, built from the crash of 1987, the recession of 1990 and 1991, the dot-com boom and bust, globalization, the housing boom and bust, the oil crisis, and the 2008 collapse of the financial markets, the worst financial upset and recession in a generation. Deep down, beneath the rocketing realities, there are important lessons to be learned, and my goal in writing this book has been to gain greater understanding of what they are and how they can be applied, personally and professionally.

A friend who worked on Wall Street, and had just seen his job and his dreams go up in smoke, expressed surprise when he learned the subject of my book. "This is the worst time to write about success," he said glumly. "We're dying out here!" I disagreed. I think there is no *better* time.

Of course, I knew where he was coming from. It's hard to talk about success when you feel like a failure. During bullish, optimistic periods, people like my friend seem to ride an upward wave with ease and confidence. The tangible evidence is right there for all to see—in their jobs, their bank accounts, their homes, their families, and the admiration of their peers. But it is a fact of life that success, once earned, is not necessarily there to stay. If ever there was a cautionary tale about the fleeting nature of success, the financial crisis of 2008 was it. We watched legendary firms at the top of their games suddenly disappear. Men and women who once seemed invincible have seen their fortunes collapse overnight. The financial services industry, which built itself into the most significant generator of profit in our times, was deflated and depleted. Everyone felt shaken. There was desperation in the air. If it had been only Lehman Brothers declaring bankruptcy, that alone would have been an unbelievable event. But bankruptcy or something close to it was also the fate of Bear Stearns, Fannie Mae, Freddie Mac, Northern Rock, Citigroup, Merrill Lynch, AIG, General Motors, Chrysler, and Wachovia: What a year!

Yet a funny thing happened in the midst of the collapse. Faced with gut-wrenching realities, many people have started to reevaluate the meaning of success, defining it in less superficial and impermanent ways. They're asking themselves hard questions that have long been ignored, about what's really important to them and where the bedrock of their personal achievement lies.

Watching the financial drama from my front-row seat at the New York Stock Exchange, where I host a daily show for CNBC called *Closing Bell*, I, too, began to assess the meaning of success—not just as an initial achievement but as a durable, lifelong pursuit. I wondered if there was a definition of success that you could have permanently, in spite of the turmoil in your life, your job, or your bank account. This question is more important than ever, given the unpredictability of the current economy. What are the intangibles that can't be measured or counted? What are the qualities that aren't reflected in your title or on your business card? And more practically, how can you remain successful even when the worst things happen to you? Is it possible to build success from failure?

The financial collapse dealt a blow to our national self-esteem. All of the old markers disappeared. As the saying goes, "Success has a thousand fathers; failure is an orphan." It's lonely at the bottom of the heap, when your BlackBerry stops buzzing and the world moves on without you. Everyone wants to be close to success, and to have success. But what is success? How do you get it, and how do you keep it?

As I reviewed my own life, I felt the urgent need to answer this question for myself. What if I woke up tomorrow and no longer had any of the external things that others (and, I admit, even I) regard as the proof that I'm doing well? Could I still look at myself in the mirror and say, "Maria, you are a success?"

I set out to answer that question.

Introduction

Seeking a
Meaningful Path

The 10 laws of success

On May 13, 2009, I stood on the field at Yankee Stadium, looking up into a sea of excited faces. It was not your usual game day, unless you were talking about the game of life. The occasion was the New York University graduation, and since Washington Square Park was under reconstruction, NYU had been allowed to use the new stadium for the event. Walking across the field, I felt a little thrill of memory and anticipation. I graduated from NYU in 1989, and it was already twenty years later. Time goes by so fast.

It was a proud and happy day. As a member of NYU's board of trustees, I was excited to be a part of the ceremonies. Wearing a cap and gown, I escorted the playwright John Patrick Shanley across the field. A 1977 graduate of NYU, he would be receiving an honorary doctorate for his award-winning play *Doubt* and his many other writing achievements.

Secretary of State Hillary Clinton delivered the commencement speech from a podium on top of second base. Here was a model of success, I thought, a woman whose titles alone were history-making—from First Lady of Arkansas to First Lady of the United States to U.S. Senator to Secretary of State. Her credibility as a role model was undeniable. It transcended politics. Hillary told the students, "This is your moment. You have made it to the big leagues and you are up to bat." And she challenged them, saying, "One of the best lines from one of my favorite baseball movies, *A League of Their Own,* said it well: 'If it were easy, anyone could do it.'" The movie she was describing was an inspiring story based on the All-American Girls Professional Baseball League, which briefly thrived as a replacement baseball league during World War II. I, too, admired that movie and loved the idea that a scrappy girls' team could capture the nation's imagination. I thought Hillary hit a perfect note in her commencement address, and the students thought so too. They cheered wildly after her remarks.

The graduating students already had the basic qualities they would need to start out on the road to success: youth, energy, brains, and optimism. But they would need other things as well—a support system of wisdom from people who had once been in their shoes. As John Patrick Shanley wrote in the preface to *Doubt,* "Life happens when the tectonic power of your speechless soul breaks through the dead habits of the mind." Those words capture the spirit of striving that is at the heart of every opportunity.

This book is my gift to the students, and to all others who seek a truly meaningful path to success in their lives. In the course of my work, I am able to interact daily with many of the great men and women of our times, and I have drawn upon their insights here. I also have had the opportunity to interview some of the most successful people in the world, to learn what makes them tick and how they achieved their happiness and success. However, when I sat down to write, I realized early on that I didn't want to merely present a collection of other people's ideas. Writing this book has forced me to recall my own experiences and to draw wisdom from them. It is written from my heart.

I've learned that although the landscape of success changes from era to era, there are fundamental qualities that remain consistent, no matter what is happening in the outside world. I have chosen ten that are the most meaningful to me—those that I believe make for success that is enduring.

1. Self-knowledge

Without self-knowledge, nothing else is possible. It's the ability to define for yourself what shape your life will take, and how you will pursue success. Success is not an abstraction. It exists in the context of who you are, where you are, and what you love. It is tangible but not necessarily monetary. It is a state of being content in your heart.

Depending on your goals, success can be holding a

degree from Harvard or holding a new baby; singing a popular song or building a popular car; feeding your family or feeding a village in a remote corner of the world; winning a prize or winning a battle with cancer; achieving a promotion or planting a garden; earning a big salary or earning the love of another person.

While you can look outward and be inspired by the examples set by others, you can't *be* them. You can only be you. In fact, your individuality is the most important foundation for success. Every successful person I've met has a strong sense of his or her unique abilities and aspirations. They're leaders in their own lives, and they dare to pursue their dreams on their own terms. They're not trying to be someone else.

2. *Vision*

Vision is the ability to look ahead and see possibility. It is the place where your dreams and your actions come together.

Vision may seem like a lofty ideal, but its most important characteristic is focus. The shotgun approach to your life and career almost never works. I once heard an older journalist counseling a young man who wanted to be a reporter but who was also pursuing a career as an actor. He told him, "As the ancient Chinese proverb goes, Man who chases two rabbits catches none." I don't know if there really is such a proverb, but the elder journalist's words rang true. Without a focused vision, you're just bouncing off walls.

Vision involves looking at the world around you and asking, "What am I going to do about it? How am I going to use the precious gift of my one life?" And then answering those questions with a plan, as did people such as Bill Gates, Hillary Clinton, and Jack Welch. The question you need to answer is how vision separates giants like them from the rest of the pack; the answer allows you to pursue your own game plan.

3. Initiative

Successful people are always thinking about what they can do to move to the next level. Initiative is the drive to do it—to take the first step, and then the next step, and then the next step. You can't *sort of* want it. You can't sit around waiting for it. My mother used to say, "The early bird gets the worm." That could be the journalist's creed, since my job is all about getting there first and going the extra mile.

The great thing about initiative is that it's free and available to everyone. It's a matter of doing something instead of not doing something. A friend of mine, an admitted procrastinator, told me that she trained herself to take initiative by committing to do one thing every day that she would normally put off—whether it was making a phone call, writing a letter, or paying a bill. She was determined

not to let her life get away from her. This simple practice,
she believed, changed her life.

4. Courage

Courage is the inner fortitude that allows you to
overcome barriers and to step up and take a
chance, even when it seems impossible. The most successful people I know embody the kind of bravery that makes
others remark, "I can't believe you did that."

An old Italian proverb says "He who does nothing
does not fail." Courage means that you'll try something
even if you aren't certain of the outcome, that you'll take a
stand when others are running for cover, that you'll risk
failure to get where you want to go. Courage isn't bravado
or taking stupid risks. It's simply deciding to live in a
mind-set of possibility instead of fear. It is manifested in
everyday actions.

5. Integrity

Integrity means doing the right thing. And what is
the right thing? I guarantee, you'll know it. You'll
feel it in your gut. Integrity means looking inside yourself.
When you strip everything else away, what kind of person
are you? When faced with an ethical dilemma, we all know
in our hearts what's the right thing to do.

Integrity has been on my mind a lot these days, because in some instances the crises in the economy were

created by a fundamental lack of integrity—decisions based on making a quick buck, regardless of whether they would improve the economy or stand the test of time. But integrity is not just reserved for the big do-or-die decisions. It's the way you behave in everyday work. And it isn't just a nice thing to have. It's also a cornerstone to success. People are attracted to integrity. If you have it, they want to be around you and to be like you. They trust you. They're willing to take a chance on you because they believe in you. You can have money and not have integrity. You can have fame and not have integrity. You can have a corner office and not have integrity. But you can never have true success without integrity.

6. *Adaptability*

Adaptability is the opposite of complacency. The survivors are always those who can adapt. That's been true since the beginning of time, and it's certainly the case now. Technology has changed so many industries, including the media, with newspapers closing down and information exploding on the web. The manufacturing sector is faltering as production and jobs are outsourced to cheaper locales. Millions of jobs have been lost, and people are wondering if they'll ever be recovered. The answer lies in our ability to adapt to change—not to resist it, but to find the openings to new opportunities. The key to adaptability is having the attitude that you've always got something to learn, even if you're at the top of the heap.

There is no question that the people who are best positioned to survive the financial crisis over the long term are those who will be adept at shifting gears.

7. *Humility*

Some of the greatest people I know are also the most humble. Humility doesn't mean being wishy-washy, or letting others run over you in their climb to the top. It's merely the understanding that you're human. People with humility are extremely appealing. We all love it when someone says, "I really screwed up." We enjoy it when people can laugh at themselves. We dislike finger-pointers and sentence parsers—those who are always looking out for their image. Without humility, you can never see the truth about yourself and others.

I grew up with the poem "If," by Rudyard Kipling. It always inspired me. "If" is in part a poem about humility—about understanding your place in the world. My favorite line is: "If you can trust yourself when all men doubt you, / But make allowance for their doubting too." In other words, believe in yourself, but don't think you're the center of the universe.

8. *Endurance*

Since success is fleeting, you can never count on keeping it once you have it. Success is a long march, and you need the tools to endure. Even if you're doing what you love, you can get burned out over time. Endurance requires pacing, discipline, and the ability to sacrifice short-term gains for long-term results. Endurance means measuring success, not as an ultimate goal at the end of the road, but as a daily fact of life. The most successful people are those who know how to pave the road with incremental triumphs.

9. Purpose

While growing up, I was in awe of the nuns who taught in my Catholic school. They possessed this mysterious thing called a "vocation." Or at least in my young mind it seemed mysterious. In those days I thought that having a calling was reserved for very special people. Now I know better. We all have a vocation, which transcends the material factors of job, income, and lifestyle. Many of the people I've met admitted that they came late to the realization of what really mattered in their lives. Usually, they were awakened because of a crisis—an illness, a job loss, or some other event that shook them to the core and forced them to look at what really mattered. But you don't have to wait for disaster to find your purpose. Deep down, we all long to live lives of meaning and fulfillment.

10. Resilience

Life is a seesaw. Sometimes you're up, sometimes you're down. In your heart of hearts, you know that success is fleeting. It's possible to lose it all—through your own actions or through circumstances beyond your control. But at times we see people coming back, almost as if they're rising from the grave, and that inspires optimism. We want to know how they did it—what attitudes and abilities allowed them to make seemingly impossible comebacks.

These ten qualities are the bedrock of enduring success. As I thought about them, a liberating realization came to me: None of the qualities are dependent on external circumstances. True success comes from the inside, meaning that anyone can have it and anyone can keep it, in good times and bad. I have always believed that you must take charge of your life; if you don't, someone will step in and do it for you. These ten qualities will help you do that regardless of the economic climate. If you draw one lesson from this book, it is that your life belongs to you, to make the most of in any way you choose. I'm just giving you a little help from some friends.

1

Self-Knowledge

Listen to your heart

If you were to ask me during the early years of my career, "Maria, what is your passion? What do you really want to do?" I wouldn't have had a good answer. I had a general idea that I wanted to pursue journalism, and I found, almost by accident, that I had an interest and facility in business reporting. But there are a thousand different ways of expressing those interests, and I was still feeling my way. Luckily, I was in the right place to figure it out.

Landing a job as a production assistant at CNN right out of college was a dream come true. I didn't even realize at first how valuable the opportunity was. When I was in school, people only wanted to work for the big guys—the established networks. But as I would discover, being at a small, non-union network like CNN allowed me a fuller plate of experiences. At the major networks, you had one job only and that was your narrow slot—whether it was teleprompting, ripping scripts, or floor direction. At CNN we all wore many hats, and I was able to learn every aspect of broadcasting.

What a time to be in the news business, especially at such an energetic young company! The Gulf War was just starting, and CNN was making history in news reporting. It was also pioneering an aggressive approach to business news, with *Money Line, Business Day,* and *Business Morning.* I was happy to go to work every day. I didn't know exactly what I wanted to do at the time, but I did know that I loved the urgency and immediacy of the news business. I also knew I had a knack for learning things by speaking to people and getting information.

Within a couple of years I had found what I felt was the right fit for me: working as an editor on the assignment desk. That doesn't sound too glamorous, I know, but I loved it. I wrote and produced pieces for on-air reporters like Kitty Pilgrim, Terry Keenan, and Jan Hopkins, who were the early stars of CNN's business division. I also worked with Lou Dobbs on his popular show, *Money Line.*

At CNN I watched and learned from many smart, hardworking newshounds who loved what they did. They knew what they were good at and adapted to a changing news business—particularly during the war, when things were moving so fast. I admired their courage as they reported from war zones in the midst of bomb blasts.

I loved my job and was completely engaged in what I was doing. And then, after five years, out of the blue, CNN announced that it was going to restructure the assignment desk. My boss presented me with the "good news" that I was being promoted from assignment editor to producer on the overnight shift. My immediate reaction was disappointment—not the usual response to a promotion. I didn't want to stop what I was doing. I was having such a great time, and I was good at interacting with sources and fostering the right relationships to get newsmakers on the air. I was beginning to compile a fantastic Rolodex. And I felt that I was valuable on the desk.

The promotion was a great opportunity, with more money and a better title, but it was not what I wanted. I was very upset, although I tried not to show it. I fled to the library on the twenty-second floor, where I could cry in peace.

It was a big moment of truth for me. Like most of my peers, I had been conditioned to think of my career as a climb up the ladder. The important thing was to keep moving upward, and it didn't matter how much you loved it as long as you nabbed the better title and the bigger paycheck. And suddenly here I was, accomplishing just that, but in my heart I knew it wasn't a job I would love. It wasn't right for me.

What to do? I wandered into the ladies' room to clean up my face, and as I stood at the sink, wiping my eyes, Kitty Pilgrim walked in. I'd always looked up to Kitty, although she was only a few years older than me. She had broken into the boys' club of business news so smoothly, and she always seemed sure of herself. To this day, Kitty remains one of the top business anchors and re-porters at CNN. I wondered how one achieved such con-fidence and certainty. I sure didn't feel it.

Noticing that I was upset, Kitty stopped to talk with me. "Kitty," I confided, "I don't know what to do. I love this place, and I don't want to leave. I'm proud to get pro-moted, but I think I will hate my new job. Should I quit? Should I just suck it up and enjoy the promotion?"

Kitty was very wise. She said, "Maria, you have to think about where you see yourself in five years. Once you get that picture, then you have to work toward it now. That's the best advice I can give you."

It was the first time anyone had spoken to me about taking the long view of my future. On that day, I began to think seriously about where I was headed. I considered what I loved—being in the center of the news, interacting with people from all walks of life, writing stories, report-ing. I also realized an aspiration I hadn't dared articulate before: to be on camera. I knew that as long as I stayed true to my ultimate goal, I could take the new job and use it as a stepping-stone to my future. And that's what I did—with a little help from the crew.

I took the new job and started producing on the overnight shift, but I now had a larger plan: to build my portfolio and on-air experience. I convinced my boss to allow me to work longer than the typical day. After my regular shift, I'd go into the field with the morning crews and pick up the news and sound bites when the markets opened. I'd write out scripts, and when I was alone with the crew, I'd ask them to shoot me on camera, reporting, so I'd have some clips. I'd wheedle and plead—"It will only take ten minutes. I have a script. Can you just shoot me?" And they were very kind and supportive. With their help, I created a portfolio of clips: "Maria Bartiromo, reporting for CNN Business News."

My heart was telling me what to do. And when I had compiled enough clips, I sent a tape to several places, including CNBC. I'd decided that I wanted to be where business news was central. And CNBC called me back. They liked my tape.

So one morning, after working all night, I got myself together and went to meet the then top executive, Peter Sturtevant, and Roger Ailes, who had just become the new president of CNBC, at their office in Fort Lee, New Jersey. I could feel that the interview was going well. We clicked. I know you can't always be sure that your instincts are right about these things, but that day, at the tender age of twenty-six, I thought I knew. I left the meeting so convinced I had the job that I went back to Manhattan and bought two new dresses.

I was exhausted by the time I got home. I had to get a few hours' sleep before I went on my night shift at CNN. In the middle of a deep sleep, I heard the phone ringing, and I grabbed it groggily. It was CNBC with an offer: they wanted me to be an on-camera reporter. I didn't go back to sleep that day. I was elated.

When I think back on that period, more than sixteen years ago, I see the journey my younger self took, and the truth I learned has stayed with me. That is, you have to know yourself and follow your heart. Titles, prestige, and money are fine, but if you don't love what you do, it's all meaningless.

Control your fate, or someone else will

Jack Welch has been an important mentor for me. When I joined CNBC in 1993, he was the chairman and CEO of our parent company, General Electric. Jack used to say, "Control your own destiny, or someone else will." (There was even a book about Jack with that title, *Control Your Destiny or Someone Else Will* by Noel Tichy and Stratford Sherman.)

It's such a basic idea—a centerpiece of success: You can't go through life thinking that the tide will just move you along and take you where you want to be. You have to swim there. In today's economic climate, I hear a lot of people saying, "I hope I don't get laid off. I hope I can hang on to my job." It's a paralyzing attitude. You might survive this storm, but what about the next one? Do you want to spend your life hoping that bad things won't happen to you? I know I don't want people working for me who are just rolling along with the tide. I want the strong swimmers—and it's okay with me if they falter sometimes, as long as they're in there kicking, moving forward.

I'm struck that one of the main characteristics of our time is the overwhelming feeling many people have that they're not in control. Many high-achieving professionals are sitting in their offices every day, hoping the phones on their desks don't ring with the dreaded summons to the head office. I have spoken with many of them, both personally and professionally. They see what's happening on Wall Street—firms consolidating and going out of business—and they're afraid they're going to be victims of the cutbacks. I notice two types of responses: Some people feel that they're trapped by circumstances and there is nothing they can do but wait and hope for the best. Others take action, improving their skills or looking for options in other fields. The big question is, How can you be like the latter group and take control of your fate in perilous times?

Here's where Kitty Pilgrim's advice is relevant. Instead of waiting for the ax to fall, and praying that it doesn't, ask yourself, "Where do I want to be in five years?" Then start moving toward your goal. Take practical steps every day. Figure out what you need. Maybe it's more training, or a broader network of colleagues and friends, or a mentor. Whatever your specific needs, be proactive.

The very act of deciding to take charge of your future helps control your emotions. It's so easy to feel like a victim, to be afraid. Fear has a ripple effect; it leads to depression. And when you're depressed, you can't be at your best, so if an opportunity does come along, you won't be ready for it. Even if you have little or no control over your circumstances, you can always control how you choose to respond. After 9/11, I had the opportunity to spend time with some of the women whose husbands worked in the towers and were among the more than three thousand people killed that day. Their initial reaction was shock and despair. In addition to the terrible emotional toll, they were also filled with fear and uncertainty about their families' financial futures. Yet they picked themselves up, and their public advocacy on behalf of victims' families became the inspiring legacy of a great tragedy. A group of the widows played a central role in pushing for the 9/11 Commission and became persistent voices for the truth about how the attacks happened and how future attacks might be prevented. These women responded to unimaginable heartbreak by deciding that their husbands' deaths would not be in vain. They elevated not only themselves but the nation. Their leadership inspired others to fight on and take action.

Make the biggest mistake of your life

Following your own path means taking risks. Maybe they'll work out, maybe they won't. When I decided to leave CNN for CNBC, I made an appointment to see my boss, Lou Dobbs, and tell him the news. He gave me a hard look and said, "Maria, you are making the biggest mistake of your life." What Lou was telling me was that he believed in me. He also believed in CNN as the best place with the most opportunities for my future. At the time CNBC was an upstart, and I'm sure Lou felt I was short-circuiting my career. It's easy to see that an opinion like that from a person you respect could send you spinning. But I had to trust myself and be willing to take my knocks if it didn't work out. It occurred to me then that Lou might be right. But I also understood that if I made decisions based on fear of failure, I would never get what I wanted in life. My taking the CNBC job wasn't a reckless act, but a decision firmly grounded on two factors: one, knowing what I wanted; and two, realizing that if it didn't work out, I could dust myself off and try another way.

You can find similar examples in the lives of most successful people—moments when the fearful chorus was screaming, "No!" But they decided to say, "Yes." Think about the heat Hillary Clinton took when she announced her plan to run for the U.S. Senate. People said she was riding on her husband's coattails, that she wasn't a "real" New Yorker, that she didn't have what it takes to be a senator. She refused to listen, and she proved them wrong. Or consider Bill Gates's decision to drop out of Harvard to focus on building the small company that became Microsoft. His family was distraught. How could he leave *Harvard,* the place of so much opportunity, to pursue what must have seemed like a pipe dream? Time proved Clinton and Gates right, but it took self-knowledge and determination for them to follow their hearts in spite of the naysayers.

I'm always intrigued when I meet successful people who made leaps into unknown territory and who had cause to ask themselves, *"What* am I doing?" before finishing the leap. I asked Eric Schmidt, the chairman and CEO of

Google, about his decision in 2001 to join the company. He was forty-six years old, nearly a generation older than the young founders, Larry Page and Sergey Brin, who were only twenty-eight. He was well established professionally, an engineer and an executive with an impressive track record. At the time he was recruited for Google, he was the CEO of the technology company Novell. The Google founders were kids embarking on an untried venture.

"Was it a big risk for you to join Google?" I asked Schmidt.

He recalled for me his first meeting with Larry and Sergey. "I walked into their office, and Larry and Sergey were standing there with a projector, and I saw a large image of my biography on the wall," he said. "And they looked like children to me. It was a very open meeting. We had a debate about what they were doing and what I was doing, and I left thinking, 'I've never met people who are so full of themselves.' But I also thought, 'I am going to see those people again, because they are really pretty special.' "

Schmidt acknowledged, "I thought at the time I was taking a terrible risk, but it was a risk that made sense because, from my perspective, I wanted to work on something really interesting. I didn't understand the search business or the advertising business. Nor did I necessarily believe Google would become a huge success." So why did he do it? He told me that what attracted him to Google was the enormous creativity of the two young men. "Brilliance often comes in a strange package," he said with a smile. "Think of Mozart or other eccentric geniuses. And I've had the privilege of working for that kind of genius in Larry and Sergey—and they're just as brilliant now as they were when they founded the company. When we started working together, I used to refer to them as 'the boys.' Today, they're no longer 'the boys.' They are seasoned veterans in technology with a very nuanced view of how to lead organizations and change the world."

And today, Eric Schmidt is very happy that he took the risk and joined Google. It has not only made him very wealthy but also very happy. He loves going to work every day.

Take money out of the equation

I recently gave a talk at Wake Forest University to students about to graduate from business school. During the discussion period, one student said, "I'm not sure what I'll do. When I decided to go to business school, everyone was telling me it was such a good idea, that it's the path that will take you to where the money is. Until the recession hit last year, I expected to start earning a high salary right after graduation. I need that salary because of my student loans, and I deserve it because of how hard I've worked. Now what am I supposed to do?" I felt for the guy. I'm sure he was very bright and capable, but I also saw him as a clear example of many students today who have lost their way. They've been following someone else's playbook for so long that they don't know how to think about their futures in anything other than monetary terms.

My first job out of school paid $18,000 a year, and it wasn't that long ago. My peers and I didn't expect to make big bucks right away. What we dreamed of was the chance to get a foot in the door, to make a start at following our dreams. Today's students have very high—and sometimes unrealistic—expectations for how they deserve to be compensated as soon as they graduate. But no one is "entitled" to make a lot of money.

After my talk, I sat down with Steven Reinemund, the former CEO of Pepsico and now the dean of the Wake Forest business school. He told me how difficult his job was because the primary way the university attracted new students was to show how many graduates landed high-paying jobs with top firms. Students thought solely in terms of the potential compensation. There's nothing wrong with wanting to make a lot of money, but its role has become far too important in the way people think about or define success. At the time of my speech, many of the top firms weren't hiring. The well had run dry. I interviewed Pepsico CEO Indra Nooyi at the university, on stage in front of students. She was very candid. I asked her what her advice was for students trying to find their way in this environment. She said it was a major opportunity. When else would you have the chance to follow your heart and take money out of the equation? She said it was time for people to look at the world, find the needs, and try to give back, and she encouraged the students to use the first year or two out of school to do good for someone in need, to volunteer, or to travel. In other words, to use the tough job market as an opportunity to stretch themselves.

Steve Reinemund was also very thoughtful about the business environment and the implications for the university. He said to me, "Business schools need to change. Currently, the best gauge we have for how well we're doing is when recruiters offer our students the highest-paying jobs. It occurs to me that this is the wrong gauge. We're encouraging students to want the most money instead of pursuing jobs based on what they love, what they're good at, and what could have a beneficial impact on the country and the world." This gauge was partly responsible for creating the bubble in financial services that burst in 2008. Talented MBAs came out of business schools, and instead of choosing careers in a variety of sectors that form the underpinnings of the economy—manufacturing, health services, technology, and the like—they headed for big money at Goldman Sachs and private equity firms like the Blackstone Group. Why? Not necessarily for love, but for money.

We began to discuss what it would mean if the measures of success for a university were tied not to how much money its graduates earned but to something deeper and more lasting. This was already beginning to happen to a certain extent, with universities like Wake Forest encouraging students to get involved in programs like Teach for America, AmeriCorps, and the Peace Corps as ways to build their résumés. Career counselors at schools could play an important role by helping students explore career options outside Wall Street.

I asked Nouriel Roubini, professor of economics at NYU's Stern School of Business, what advice he would give to students coming out of school today that would set them on a course for success. Nouriel is incredibly astute. A full two years before the financial collapse of 2008, he predicted that the United States was headed for a major housing bust, an oil crisis, and a recession that would create a seismic shock in the world economy. Few people gave his predictions credence. The *New York Times* nicknamed him "Dr. Doom." Today Nouriel has been proved right. While his message isn't always easy to hear, he's one of those rare people who has his finger on the pulse of the economy. Nouriel believes that students shouldn't go into finance, but instead should share the wealth of their knowledge and experience in other fields. "I think this country needs more people who are going to be entrepreneurs, more people in manufacturing, more people going into sectors that will lead to long-term economic growth," he told me. "When the best minds of the country are all going to Wall Street, there is a distortion in the allocation of human capital that eventually becomes inefficient."

Nouriel's point is crucial: We must reevaluate what success means and how we talk about success, especially to the young people who are making decisions about their futures. Over the past twenty-five years, the financial services arena has grown in importance, becoming a dominant part of our economy. It has a tremendous allure, with most of the talented people coming out of business school headed into financial careers where they are very highly paid. They were no longer considering the broad scheme of the economy and looking at careers in manufacturing, biotech, and other bedrock industries. Now we've had a shock to the financial system. The allure is gone, and so are the jobs.

I always tell students, "Don't go into an industry because you feel that you're going to get rich from it. Don't take a job because you think that's the best money you can make. Always take a job because you love what you do. The money can follow, but if you don't love what you do, you're going to be miserable. And if you're not happy, you're not going to want to work."

And now I challenge students to take it one more step: "Imagine if all jobs paid the same. What would you want to do with your life?"

I invite you to ask yourself that question now. Be honest. If you took money out of the equation, what would be your ideal profession? If it's different from what you're actually doing or training to do, you face a serious dilemma—a conflict of self-interest. In that case, measure the distance between your aspirations and your reality, and start taking action to narrow the gap. How much are you willing to sacrifice to do the work you love? It's fine to have aspirations that include financial success. After all, a key premise of capitalism is the opportunity to prosper, no matter where you start out. On the other hand, if you study the backgrounds of the most prosperous people in society today, you'll see stories of achievement from the ground up. Oprah Winfrey started out as a local radio reporter in Tennessee. Steven Spielberg began his career as an unpaid intern at Universal Studios. Former Hewlett-Packard CEO Carly Fiorina worked for years as a secretary at financial firms. Warren Buffett was an investment salesman in Omaha. Ron Meyer, now the head of Universal, started out as his boss's driver. There are hundreds of similar examples. Today, because their lives seem magical, it's easy to forget how they got there.

"Where you are from is not who you are"

These are the words that Ursula Burns heard repeatedly from her mother when she was a young kid growing up in a poor neighborhood on the Lower East Side of Manhattan. Today Ursula is the CEO of Xerox Corporation and is the first African American woman to lead a Fortune 500 company. She is an important role model for those from humble beginnings who aspire to greatness.

Ursula credits her success to performance—her engineering talent has been on display at Xerox for almost thirty years—not to gender or race. Her ability to be an innovative thinker, she told me, stems from her life story, one that is very different from that of most executives at

Xerox. "Coming from a place that is different from the norm helps to make that a natural way to approach problems or opportunities," she told me. "I was born and raised in the Lower East Side of Manhattan to a single mother. And that for me is normal. Most of the leaders in the industry come from a different background than I do, so my unique perspective adds value to my contribution. I have always seen it that way. And Xerox is a great place for a person like me, because it values individuality." Ursula is referring to the fact that Xerox was at the forefront of employee diversity programs as early as the 1960s, and she was a beneficiary of those efforts. Today, one-third of Xerox's executives are women, an impressive statistic in corporate America. In Ursula's view, diversity—the combined life experiences of people from different backgrounds—enhances the makeup and potential of a company. Rather than fighting against her roots and their associated disadvantages, she views them as inherent to her successful journey.

Oprah Winfrey also stands out as an example of a woman who found the secret to success by just being herself. Dennis Swanson, now with the Fox network, has been credited with "discovering" Oprah back when he was the general manager of the ABC affiliate in Chicago. He told me that Oprah was a young woman who didn't fit into the conventional TV mold, but she wanted to break into television. He gave her a job reading news, and it just didn't work. She was awkward and stiff, and she definitely didn't look the part. But Dennis saw something in her. He said,

"Oprah, don't read the teleprompter. Just be yourself and show me what's in your heart." That's what she did, and she blew everyone away. Dennis remembers Oprah asking him, "How did I do?" He replied, "All I can tell you is when you go home tonight and get feedback from your friends and family, be sure to keep your head on straight because we need it to fit through the door when you come to work tomorrow." Oprah was an instant success by being herself.

Acknowledging your roots and being true to yourself is a powerful foundation. Every single successful person I spoke to in the course of writing this book mentioned that. I know where they're coming from, because it has been my own experience. As a child in Bay Ridge, I never imagined that my face would be on billboards. I could not have predicted that leaders in politics, finance, and science would be answering my phone calls, meeting with me, and asking for my opinions. I wasn't sitting in my kindergarten classroom imagining a television career. But, like Ursula Burns, my path was being formed by the constant message coming from my parents and teachers: "Where you are from is not who you are." And yet equally important is never forgetting how you achieved what you have and where you come from. I am so proud of my Italian American background, where hard work and values were the foundations of success. It is one of the reasons, no matter how busy I am at work or traveling, I try hard to give back to this community. I regularly host the Columbus Day weekend parade and gala because of my love of my heritage.

Be the only you

When I speak with people in the entertainment industry, I sometimes feel they radiate an underlying worry. It's especially true of women. They're looking at the younger women coming behind them, always conscious that they have a shelf life—an end point when they'll no longer be able to attract the same kind of attention. This mentality is pervasive in our culture, and it isn't just among entertainers. But all of us in television feel the pressure with unusual intensity. I have been inspired by so many women, but two that stand out are Goldie Hawn and Mary Hart, who have demonstrated remarkable cool in the face of the pressure.

I met Goldie a few years ago at *Fortune* magazine's annual "Most Powerful Women in Business" conference. She was one of the inspirational speakers, and she also led a yoga class, which I took. We hit it off and became friendly, e-mailing and getting together when we could. Goldie is a delight to be around. At sixty-three, she exudes a youthfulness and a positive spirit. Over dinner one night I asked her, "How have you stayed successful in Hollywood, when there are younger, fresher faces wanting what you have?" She laughed. "That reminds me of a line I had in a movie: 'Everybody wants to be me.' What movie *was* that?"

When you've made so many movies, it can be hard to keep track. I supplied the answer—*First Wives Club*—and we laughed. Then, turning serious, Goldie said, "Maria, it's very simple. There are many people who eventually will come along and try to be 'me' or to replace me. It doesn't matter. I just focus on what I'm doing, because that's what I can control." Goldie is comfortable in her own skin. She knows that if she starts watching her back, she'll collide with what's ahead. She told me that she hasn't made a movie in seven years because she wants to do what makes her happy, and she only looks at scripts that truly interest her. She finds tremendous fulfillment in her family—including her partner of twenty-six years, Kurt Russell, and her children, Kate, Oliver, and Wyatt. She has also started a foundation whose mission is promoting the emotional health and well-being of children. One thing I know about Goldie: She will always be herself, fully and happily. She likes herself, and she doesn't try to be anyone else.

Mary Hart, at fifty-eight, is gorgeous, powerful, and relevant. She continues to be the popular host of *Entertainment Tonight*. I recently said to Mary, "I can't believe you've been doing this for as long as you have, since entertainment is such a youth-oriented business. Let's face it: How many cute young blondes want to be you?" She laughed at that, and said, "They're always going to throw younger, fresher kids at you to make you feel insecure. I don't think about it. I'm doing what I'm doing, and my viewers know me, and the newcomers are not me. I'm the only me!" That really hit home: *I'm the only me.* Sure, there will always be others who have qualities you don't have. But when you're comfortable with yourself and can appreciate your special qualities, no one can ever supplant you.

I realize that you may be skeptical about the advice to be yourself, perhaps thinking it's a tough thing when you're just getting started, and especially difficult if you work in a large company. One of the reasons I appreciated Jack Welch so much when he was running GE was that he let us know that individual creativity thrilled him. He was famous for sending personal notes to people who did something smart or innovative. As the recipient of several of his notes, I can tell you it was a real confidence booster. But Jack told me that the notes weren't just a tactic to boost employee morale. "It turned me on to write them as much as it turned them on to receive them," he said. Jack viewed his role as comparable to an orchestra leader. "An orchestra has basses. It has violins," he said. "And the leader's job is to touch every one of those people so they know they're free to think and do things better."

Herb Kelleher, the charismatic cofounder of Southwest Airlines, is widely admired for creating a culture of individuality. He described it to me in simple terms: "We tell our employees, 'Be yourself. Have fun. Don't be afraid to do what you want to do. We hired you because you're you. We don't want you to come to work looking like a robot or an automaton. We want you to be yourself at work.'" It has been a winning formula for the airline.

Sometimes it takes extra effort to be yourself—and to find out who your self really is. When I interviewed Bill

Ford, I was struck by the fact that although he had special opportunities by virtue of his heritage, carrying the Ford family name and legacy also presented special challenges. He had to find a way to create his own identity and make his own mark on the company. He had to ask himself, "How can I make an original contribution?" Bill was not interested in being a caretaker. He became the first American auto executive to aggressively pursue green technology. "I've been an environmentalist my whole life," he told me, "and I've fought a lot of battles during thirty years at Ford. In fact, when I first went on the board, I was told I had to stop associating with any known or suspected environmentalists. And I said, 'No, of course I have no intention of stopping.' I was viewed as a bit of a Bolshevik throughout my whole career." Against the odds, Bill Ford persisted, rebuilding the iconic Rouge plant as the greenest plant on the planet and launching the first American hybrid, the Escape. By following his personal instincts, even in the face of resistance, Bill Ford made an indelible mark on an iconic company.

Successful business leaders understand that people really do matter—not just in the cold "human resources" sense, but as individuals with all their unique styles and passions and approaches to life. Once you understand that, you have the permission and the power to go places no one has gone before and to imagine opportunities that didn't previously exist.

Stay true to yourself through the transitions

I spent some time talking with Condoleezza Rice when she was secretary of state, as well as after she left office. She is an impressive woman—smart, self-confident, and global-minded. What makes Condi so successful, though, is that she never forgets where she came from. She is down-to-earth and humble. She speaks movingly about growing up in Birmingham, Alabama, where her parents bridged two worlds. They lived through the worst years of segregation, yet they were educated, progressive people who recognized that change was in the air. They raised Condi to live, not in the old world, but in the new world that was yet to be. In essence, they raised her on an act of faith, and their faith paid off. Condi constantly expresses gratitude for her upbringing, and for the love and support that propelled her while also keeping her grounded.

When I interviewed Condi shortly before she left office, I was very curious about how she would handle her change in status. I've always wondered about the experience of going from a high-profile position in a presidential administration to life as a private citizen. It must be difficult. One day you're meeting with foreign leaders, traveling the world, having a huge impact on the future of our country and others. The next day you're watching someone else take the reins. Condi admitted that it was an emotional time for her, coming to the end of her tenure with the Bush administration. But she was clear that being secretary of state was not the only role that defined her; she still had her identity and passions, just as she always had.

Condi told me, "I'm an educator at heart. I'm someone who believes in the transformative power of education. I've seen it in my own life. I know that education is the way to a better life." Reflecting on her time in office, she said, "What is most admired about America is that you can come from modest circumstances and do extraordinary things. But you can't do them without the benefit of education."

In the coming years, Condi plans to be a force for opportunity in education. She doesn't see it as a divergent path from her role in government. In fact, she is the first to insist that she is not a politician.

What impresses me about Condi is her enthusiasm for the next stage of her journey and her strong sense of identity. She doesn't view the change in her circumstances as a jarring, dissonant note. She is not wistful about the past. Like the classically trained pianist she is, Condi Rice is going seamlessly from one movement to the next, understanding that each period of her life is part of a complete symphony.

Take it personally

You may not own the company, but you own your life. Maybe the job you have now is not the one you really want, but you have to inhabit it every day, take it personally, and know that what you do makes a difference. I learned that lesson very early in life. During high school I had a job at a bridal shop. I told myself, "Sure, carrying around heavy dresses will earn me money, but trying them on and visualizing my own wedding one day is more fun." I didn't take the job seriously enough, and I screwed around. I'd try on dresses and get distracted. Well, it may not have been important to me, but it was sure important to the customers. I got fired, and I was devastated. I cried. How could they fire me? It was pretty simple: they needed someone who could own the job, not just hang out.

I always tell the writers on my shows, "The words you're sending out over the air are going to have an impact. People are going to base important decisions on those words. Never forget that." When I have a project to assign, I don't hand it to the person who is just marking time. I look for the one who will take it personally.

When I interviewed Sir Martin Sorrell, the British businessman and CEO of WPP Group, the world's largest advertising agency, he told the story of how he learned what it meant to take work personally. Martin told me that he came late to his passion. "At the age of forty, when I was having my male menopause—or I think what's technically called andropause—and looking back at what I'd done and what I wanted to do, I decided to go off on my own," he explained. "I started WPP with two other people in a one-room office. It was as near as a man could get to having a baby, certainly not physically, but psychologically and emotionally. And this is a key to success—having an attachment to the business, a love for the business, and a passion for the business that a founder has. You are most successful in life when you are having fun at what you are doing. It may sound trite, but if you set out to make a lot of money, my experience is you'll be unsuccessful. But when you set out to follow your heart and dreams, you become a sort of natural success story. You want to spend all of your time doing it. I don't think people are successful because they make a million dollars, or a hundred million dollars, or a billion dollars. That is just keeping score. I think you have to be comfortable in your own skin. I am a founder and when you are a founder, you have an attachment and love for the business and a passion for the business like no one else. It's not a job you are hired for. It's 24/7 and you take it all personally. I have loved the challenge of new media, of the consumer insight and building a business from scratch." Martin's business, which started with two people, now has 133,000 people, $7 billion in market value, and operations in 106 countries.

"The best way I can put it," Martin added, "is the way Bill Shankly, a famous coach in the U.K., did. Shankly managed the Liverpool Football Club, and he used to say, 'Football is not a matter of life and death. It's more important than that.' And so, WPP to me is not a matter of life and death; it's more important than that. Everything that happens in my company I take personally."

That's also what drives Chris Gardner, the CEO of Gardner Rich & Co., whose remarkable story was the sub-

ject of the hit Will Smith movie *The Pursuit of Happyness*.
Chris went from being a struggling salesman to losing his
home to founding a multimillion-dollar Chicago investment firm—all while honoring a promise to always be
there for his son. A series of bad breaks left him homeless
at one point. He had interviewed at every firm on Wall
Street and finally been accepted into the Dean Witter
training program, but he wasn't the most polished candidate. He still didn't have a permanent home. I asked
him, "Did anybody at work in the Dean Witter training
program know about your dire situation? Did people
know there were nights that you actually slept under your
desk?"

"No," he answered, "and they did not need to know.
What they needed to know was that I showed up at work
every day and I lit it up. Every day I started out in this
business doing retail brokerage. And that level of the
business is all about numbers. That meant two hundred
phone calls a day. I knew that every time I picked up the
phone, I was digging my way out of a hole and creating a
better life for my children."

When I asked him the secret to his success, Chris said,
"I honest to God believe, with all of my heart, that you've
got to find something you absolutely love. Something that
gets you so excited that you cannot wait for the sun to
come up in the morning because you want to go do your
thing. Money is the least significant aspect of wealth. I've
got one problem right now, Maria, that some of the richest
people in the world do not have. And that is, I cannot sleep

at night because my face hurts from walking around smiling all day."

Beat the stereotype

I've probably been asked a thousand times what it's like to be a woman reporting on the male-dominated finance industry. It's a fair question. If you walk around the floor of the New York Stock Exchange, you'll still see very few women in the sea of dark suits. One of my colleagues at CNBC joked, "I think ninety-nine percent of the women at the Exchange work for us." The barriers to being a woman on Wall Street are real, but I've always believed that I could work through them and even enjoy the challenge.

I like the way Meredith Whitney, one of the sharpest banking analysts around, put it. She is a former managing director of Oppenheimer & Co. and now runs her own firm, the Meredith Whitney Advisory Group. Meredith has the uncanny ability (and the accompanying nerve) to get ahead of the trends, and she isn't afraid to have unpopular views. She got out in front on predicting the troubles of Citigroup and other banks, and she took a lot of heat for it before her predictions were vindicated by what happened during the meltdown. "As far as being a woman in this industry," Meredith told me, "it doesn't matter if you're a toad if you've got good ideas and you can make people money." That's the truth. Like me, Meredith tries to focus on the work and ignore the chatter. "Ultimately it just comes down to work ethic and not being scared to take chances," she said. "People are starved for good research in a bad market, and I'm consumed by all of this. I'm not getting a lot of sleep, but you've got to strike while the iron is hot."

That's not to say that women don't have extra distractions to deal with. People love to gossip, especially about the way we look. But the fact is, you don't get anywhere in your profession unless you know your stuff. Good looks might open some doors, especially when you're in media or entertainment, but it's the *goods*— knowledge, experience, and work ethic—that will keep you there. Assessing women based on their looks is similar to the compartmentalizing of any group. Take the elevation in 2009 of the first Latina Supreme Court justice, Sonia Sotomayor. Marc H. Morial, president and CEO of the National Urban League, made an interesting comment about her appointment to the court. He told me that while it is an important historical milestone, it is Justice Sotomayor's distinguished record of academic excellence, legal expertise, and outstanding judicial performance, not her race or gender, that are the strongest testament to the hope that millions of children will achieve their dreams if they persevere, no matter where they start in life.

I'm proud to have broken some barriers in business news, and I know I did it not because of the way I looked, or even because of my gender, but because I worked and studied hard, learned my craft, and was resourceful. Period.

Create your own measures of success

Success means different things to different people, so you have to figure out what it means for you. Recently, I was reading about how Oprah Winfrey was disappointed in herself because she had put on weight. And you might say, wait a minute—she's *Oprah*. She has everything in the world. How can she use weight to measure her success? Well, obviously Oprah has other measures of success too, but I understood how she felt, and I sure know what it's like to put on a few pounds while the world watches. We all have certain markers for ourselves, and weight is one Oprah puts in place to gauge her personal success. At the end of the day, only you know how you're living your life. Only you know if you're measuring up to your own standards. Only you know if you feel right in your skin.

Here is a useful exercise when you're thinking about your own success. If you accept the fact that you are in charge of your destiny, ask yourself, what are your personal measures? If you can answer that question, it will protect you and give you a sense of control during tough times, when the rug gets pulled out from under you.

There are two keys to considering your personal measures of success. The first is that they should be achievable. If you're five foot two, you wouldn't say, "I'd be successful if I played for the NBA." Again, self-knowledge is important. The second key is that, to the extent possible, your measures should come from inside.

So name your success measures. Write them down. Look at them at the end of each week and evaluate whether your actions, attitudes, and achievements of the week were true to your core. Turn off the judgments of others and look inside. If you get in the habit of doing this every week, soon it will become second nature.

In the course of your life and career, the goalposts will change many times, but with self-knowledge the central goalpost—who you really are and what you aspire to—will remain steady.

2

Vision

*Plant your dreams
on solid ground*

On January 20, 2009, I had the opportunity to be in Washington, D.C., for the inauguration of Barack Obama. It was a brutally cold day, but you'd never have known it from the throngs of people on the streets. They were happy, smiling, full of camaraderie. I had never before witnessed such a visceral sense of optimism. If you were to take a snapshot of that single day, you'd have to come away saying, "How wonderful to be an American." It wasn't a political statement, just a spontaneous eruption of pride.

Observing the event, I thought, "This is what the perception of visionary leadership can do." And even though that spectacular day has been followed by the tough realities of a tumbling economy and a nation still at war, the perception of a new course of action led by a vision triggered pride and commitment across the nation. Vision rallies people. No matter what your individual politics, on that day everyone could feel a camaraderie, a sense of belief in the hope that President Obama's vision gave us.

Vision as a quality of success isn't just for world leaders. It can be found and cultivated in your own backyard. Vision is more than rhetoric; it's deeper than charisma. It is the quality that enables you to be creative, passionate, inspired, and productive. With one eye on the future, it keeps you grounded in the practical actions of the present.

During the 2008 race for the Democratic nomination, some people ridiculed Barack Obama over a story that he supposedly started planning to run for president when he was in kindergarten. While kindergartners don't engage in that kind of long-term thinking, it's obvious that Obama had a vision for his life from a young age. Ignoring the difficult circumstances of his upbringing, he looked ahead and plotted a course to get where he wanted to be. We can all do that.

Ask what your life is preparing you for

January 2009 marked another unforgettable event. On January 15, U.S. Airways Flight 1549, headed from New York City to Charlotte, North Carolina, struck a flock of geese and suffered total engine failure just minutes after takeoff. The now famous pilot, Chesley ("Sully") Sullenberger, fifty-seven, landed the plane in the icy waters of the Hudson River. Since every passenger on board was safely rescued, the incident came to be known as the Miracle on the Hudson.

Several days later I was having dinner with Garry Kasparov. Garry and I had met at a conference nearly a decade earlier, and we became good friends. Garry constantly impresses me with his thoughtfulness, his courage, and his wonderful instincts. A world-champion chess player, with a heroic status in Russia, he has used his fame to become a political activist in his native country. After he was arrested at an anti-Putin rally in 2007, I asked Garry, "Why do you keep putting your life on the line in Russia? You have a house in America. You have a wife and daughter here. You have resources to do anything you want to do." He responded simply, "Maria, I have to. I love my country." That's Garry.

On this evening in January 2009, Garry and I were talking about the "miracle on the Hudson." Garry said, "Sully's whole life prepared him for that moment."

His comment stopped me short. What an interesting— and undeniably true—perspective. Sully had been an airline pilot for thirty years, and before that a fighter pilot. He wasn't that far from retirement. He'd never had an accident. And in a flash, a lifetime of experience, practice, wisdom, and inner fortitude came into play, with an amazing result. Sully could never have envisioned that moment, or prepared for it, but when life presented a life-or-death challenge, he acted.

Long after my dinner with Garry, his words lingered. I began to wonder what my life was preparing me for, and I found it an exhilarating question. I think everyone should contemplate it. Now obviously there are some professions—like being an airplane pilot, a police officer, or a soldier—when everything can change in an instant and you have to be ready to act. But preparing for the unexpected, and then acting decisively, should be an important part of everyone's training and life experience. You never know when you'll face a moment of crisis. I think of the Virginia Tech professor Liviu Librescu, a seventy-six-year-old Holocaust survivor, who put himself between the shooter and his students during the 2007 campus massacre. He saved their lives, but lost his. Professor Librescu had a brutal training ground in Nazi-occupied Romania, but it is doubtful that he ever expected violence to enter his American classroom. Most professions don't include training for the unexpected, but maybe they should.

The ability to act quickly in the face of sudden upheaval is a component of vision. Vision is a big word, and it's often seen as a lofty concept. But in practice, vision is about the small stuff—the daily actions that keep you moving in top form toward your larger goal. In interviews, Sully has repeatedly said that he was just doing his job. But that's exactly when life happens. Vision is having a plan. It is difficult to lead a team and have success without beginning with a vision.

Cultivate wisdom

The world has changed. The recent financial crisis caught us off guard. Most people have not lived through this kind of financial distress before, and shifting gears to the new reality is hard to do. In the midst of the financial shock waves I hosted a dinner for my top boss, Jeff Immelt, the chairman and CEO of General Electric. About twenty of the nation's chief investors were at the dinner. They were facing the toughest economic period any had ever seen, and I wanted to know how everyone was feeling and what they thought would happen next. Needless to say, there was lively conversation around the table, but the general tone was mostly what we've all heard before. One person remarked that the markets will go up and the markets will go down, but they will eventually stabilize. Another said we had to hold on for the long term. Still another said the stock market's history proved it ultimately had the best returns over other arenas. All the comments were typical of what experts say during any market event.

And then Michael Steinhardt, the prominent investor, hedge fund manager, and philanthropist (who is also the chairman of my husband's company, WisdomTree), spoke in a very low voice. Although his words were softly stated, they had more impact than anything else that had been said. "Where," Michael asked, "is the wisdom at this table? We are in a period that is unlike any we have seen before. It's not the same as the last time. And the solutions are not going to be the same. What are we going to do to address the fact that it's different? Where's the outside-the-box thinking?"

Everyone at the table was stopped short by Michael's comments, and the conversation shifted to address his point. I can't say there were any solutions unearthed at the dinner party, but thanks to Michael, at least we were considering the new reality instead of relying on outdated assumptions.

Later, after some reflection, I started to understand that I had been struggling to make sense of the financial crisis using the old paradigms. This new reality was completely foreign to me because I had lived through a bull market for much of my career. Free-market capitalism was working just fine for all those years. Given my experience, when crisis struck, it was very hard for me to acknowledge that the old rules might no longer apply. I had to challenge myself to think beyond the familiar assumptions.

Paradoxically, while changing times require a new vision, we also need to draw on the lessons of history. We have such short memories! The minute a crisis ends, we slide right back into the comfortable old behaviors. It's like surviving a hurricane and thinking there will never be another one. Since 1999 we have seen four bubbles pop: dot-com, oil, housing, and finance. We were shocked each time, but have we learned the right lessons? Do we fully understand the origins of each crisis? Look at housing. While housing prices were soaring, everyone treated it as if fairy dust had been sprinkled over neighborhoods across America. Prices just kept going up, but why? Were there better roads? Better schools? More desirable houses? No, it was all based on a speculative fever. Now, as the housing market begins slowly coming back, how can we prevent it from unraveling again? One obvious way is for individuals to reject the smoke and mirrors, to use our wisdom to make realistic choices. Renowned international investor and financial commentator Jim Rogers once told me, "Always be a contrarian. Question what the herd is saying and doing." Remember the old obvious wisdom: If it looks too good to be true, it probably is. If you consider the 2008 financial crisis and the earlier dot-com bust, you'll notice they had two things in common: both were preceded by extended periods of euphoria—a sense that things were just going to keep getting better and better— and there were few contrarians around to bring people down to earth. Everyone was swept up in the euphoria.

On a micro level, our attitudes about credit had not only contributed to a systemic breakdown, they had poisoned the personal opportunities of thousands of individuals. Credit card debt is an example of a collapse of wisdom. Credit cards are false spending power. They are funny money. They are the lie we tell ourselves that we can afford to spend more than we have. I am not a fan of credit cards, and I rarely use them. If I want to buy something, I pull out my debit card, which has a true relationship to the money I have in the bank.

The psychology behind credit card activity is the same flawed attitude behind the systemic bubble that nearly broke our financial system. Clearly, we need a new model of consumer opportunity. You can participate in creating that new model by being on your toes and looking beyond the façades. Whether you are a student examining your prospects, a veteran of the workplace planning your next step, a consumer buying a house, or an investor trying to understand the market, stop and ask yourself some basic questions: How has the landscape of success changed? What has ended, and what is beginning? What is sound, and what is too good to be true? Study the evidence of the past. What have you learned about why systems and people rise and fall, and how can you apply it to your own circumstances? Are you living in a bubble of outlandish expectations? Are you spending what you don't have? Use your wisdom to keep your feet on the ground.

Have an inquiring mind

Bill and Melinda Gates have a home overlooking Seattle's Lake Washington that has many awe-inspiring features. But the centerpiece, intellectually and emotionally, is the library. When you walk into this enormous room, with its hand-carved bookshelves and domed ceiling, you feel as if you are walking into history. There is not a computer in sight. Instead, there are the artifacts of great men of the past—a copy of Lincoln's Emancipation Proclamation, the papers of Leonardo da Vinci, and the letters of Benjamin Franklin, including the one in which he wrote, "Early to bed and early to rise, makes a man healthy, wealthy and wise."

I was standing in the library not long ago, taking it all in and thinking how emblematic it was of the man himself. The occasion of my visit was Bill's annual technology summit for CEOs. I had been invited to chair a panel on the future of the economy. Although Bill has now stepped down from active leadership in Microsoft to concentrate on his foundation, he is still a leader in the industry he loves.

As magnificent as his physical surroundings may be, the man himself is the standout. I have interviewed Bill on a number of occasions, and I always come away thinking that he is on another level from most people I have met in my life. For that I credit his intense interest in every topic that comes up. This quality was on full display as we gathered at his home for dinner. In a room full of the leaders of business and industry, Bill's voice rose above the rest— at one moment talking about corporate tax rates, at another alternative energy, at another the future of technology, at another the crisis of malaria in Africa.

He is out to change the world, and he is succeeding because of his intense curiosity and a mind that never stops asking how to do things better. He is a mental tinkerer who loves an intellectual challenge, whether it is the design of a new software program, inventing a refrigeration system for safe delivery of malaria drugs, or beating his friend Warren Buffett at a game of bridge. He surrounds himself with other curious minds, and those who aspire to work at Microsoft or at the Bill and Melinda Gates Foundation must have similar levels of passion and intensity.

This quality of intense curiosity doesn't come as naturally to everyone, but it can be developed. You can start by stepping beyond your comfort zone, surrounding yourself with people whose experiences are different from yours, reading outside your field, and talking to people whom you disagree with. You can challenge your own assumptions about what is possible and what you believe. You can keep tinkering.

Imagine a different world

In 2009 Bill Gates Sr. wrote a book of inspiration and reflections titled *Showing Up for Life: Thoughts on the Gifts of a Lifetime*. He asked his son to write the foreword. A mere two sentences, it says it all:

> *Dad, the next time somebody asks you if you're the real Bill Gates, I hope you say, "Yes." I hope you tell them that you're all the things the other one strives to be.*

It's a touching tribute, and well deserved. Bill Sr. doesn't command much public attention, and he likes it that way. But when I interviewed him in May 2009, I recognized that this down-to-earth eighty-three-year-old man has been the quiet, behind-the-scenes engine of the Gates Foundation from its early days. As I spoke with him, it all came together for me—how the seed of his son's altruistic spirit was planted in childhood and passed on by his parents and grandmother, who always felt driven to understand and respect their role in the world.

Born in 1925, Bill Sr. was a child of the Great Depression. "I lived in Bremerton [a community across Puget Sound from Seattle], and like everywhere else, we were in terrible trouble," he told me. "There were huge numbers of people out of work, shantytowns were popping up around the area to house the homeless and destitute, and it seemed that no one was immune. In that atmosphere, I inevitably learned that sometimes the only thing separating the poor from others was chance or luck. And that led me to see that I, too, had the potential to be poor."

Pretty profound thinking for a kid. This understanding and upbringing laid the foundation for an egalitarian philosophy that was then passed on to his children.

Bill Sr. spent his career practicing law, and he was successful in his own right, weaving philanthropy through his professional activities. He and his wife, Mary (who died in 1994), taught their three children—Kristi, Bill, and Libby—to be community-minded. "Both Mary and I grew up in families where this was part of the way things were," he said. "We saw our parents contributing to their communities, so that was something we were used to and accepted as the way we would be with our children. Kristi, Bill, and Libby grew up with the sense that it was the way the world worked. Good people shared."

Fast-forward from that learning to the creation of the William H. Gates Foundation (later called the Bill and Melinda Gates Foundation). Bill Sr. remembers it well: "It was the fall of 1994, at a time when I was tapering off in my practice. We were standing in line at a theater, and Bill was telling me how difficult it was to keep up with all of the charitable requests coming to Microsoft. So we made a deal. I said, 'You send me the letters and the requests, and I'll come around and talk to you once a month or so, and we'll work it out.' That was what we were going to do. But within a week he called me and said, 'Dad, as a result of our conversation the other night, Melinda and I have decided that we are going to start a foundation.'" His main concern was that he wouldn't have the time, and Bill Sr. stepped in to fill the gap. The initial contribution from Microsoft was $100 million.

I was curious about this quiet family that took on some of the biggest problems in the world. Yes, they had the resources, but actually making things happen requires more than just funding. How did they conceive their vision? How did they choose where to put their energy and money?

Bill Sr. told me that in the beginning "we didn't have any particular purpose in mind. We were just going to do a good citizen kind of philanthropy, like several others in town. And we were only thinking locally. A couple of incidents occurred which changed that dramatically—principally, the time that Bill and Melinda read a *New York Times* article about the egregious disparity between health care in the poor world and in the developed world, and how millions of people were dying of things that weren't even a problem in the United States and other Western nations. And it really hit them very dramatically. They said,

'Dad, maybe we could do something about this.' And I said, 'By all means.' So that was a big turning point."

From this realization came the core philosophy of the Bill and Melinda Gates Foundation: "All lives are created equal." Once they internalized that conviction, their foundation's vision came into focus. They could imagine a different world, and they have set about to realize that goal with donations of about $1.5 billion a year.

Bill and Melinda have internalized a profound sense of the equality of all people, a fact that Bill demonstrated quite vividly while speaking to a technology, entertainment, and design conference in February 2009. Standing before a packed room filled with the stars of technology, politics, and entertainment, he spoke passionately about his foundation's efforts to end the plague of malaria in Africa. The crowd listened politely; they had all heard such speeches before. Bill thought they needed a more practical demonstration. "Malaria is spread by mosquitoes," he said, holding up a jar of mosquitoes. "I brought some. Here. I'll let them roam around. There is no reason only poor people should be infected." And he pulled off the lid, releasing the flying bugs into the room. The crowd let out a gasp of shock. Bill hastened to say that these mosquitoes were not malaria carriers, but he hoped to create a "there but for the grace of God" experience for his privileged audience. He was stretching their imaginations and putting them, for a moment, in the place of those for whom the sight of a mosquito was a real danger. In doing so, he was also offering them a vision of a different world.

Be an inspiration

In March 2009, I was at the G-20 summit in London and I witnessed many remarkable events. But one that especially captivated me happened outside the conference, when First Lady Michelle Obama visited the Elizabeth Garrett Anderson Language School in North London and appeared before two hundred inner-city girls. The First Lady spoke with genuine emotion, saying, "All of you are jewels and you touch my heart. It is important for the world to know that there are wonderful girls like you all over the world." And realizing how many barriers these girls would have to overcome in their lives, she reminded them of her own roots. "Nothing in my life's path would have predicted that I would be standing here," she told the girls. "I am an example of what is possible when girls, from the very beginning of their lives, are loved and nurtured by the people around them. We are counting on every single one of you to be the best that you can be. We know you can do it. We love you." And then she delivered warm hugs to as many of the girls as she could reach.

Watching Michelle Obama, I realized once again just how powerful our words can be—how eager young people are to be inspired and to hear that they have potential, no matter where they come from. I'm certain that many of those girls will never forget the American First Lady's words—that ten or twenty years from now, we will be hearing from them as they look back on that day and cite it as the moment they knew they could accomplish anything.

Another example of tremendous inspiration is Queen Rania of Jordan. Although she lives in a part of the world that isn't always open to equality for women, she has aggressively promoted the rights and empowerment of women and children. She is truly an international role model. She has often said, "As you educate a young woman, you educate the family. If you educate the girls, you educate the future."

Inspiring words can have a transforming effect on individuals and on the whole culture. They're not empty if there is substance behind them. A friend once told me, "Martin Luther King didn't say, 'I have a business plan.' He said, 'I have a dream.'" His dream was the vision of equality. And as Dr. King made clear, once you know where you want to go, you can begin to take others there.

Imagine the impact each of us can have on emerging generations. Every day we have the opportunity to reach out and truly make a difference in a young person's life. In the most mundane moments, we can hand out possibility. It's within our power. Think back. All of us can point to someone whose words changed our lives.

Here's a secret I've learned: You don't have to be at the top of the heap to be an inspiration. No matter where you stand, chances are there are people who look up to you. If you are a young businessperson, go back to your alma mater and speak to the students. If you are a college

student, go back to your high school. If you are an entrepreneur, reach out in your community. Become the person
others remember. Help them create their own vision.

Solve the next problem

Nell Merlino has devoted her life to solving problems for women. She is an enormously creative
thinker whose ideas, such as Take Our Daughters to Work
Day, have become a part of the fabric of America. Nell has
the ability to focus like a laser on an underlying problem
to find a practical solution. In 1999 she cofounded Count
Me In for Women's Economic Independence, an online
service to give women entrepreneurs a leg up with loans,
advice, and education. But it really nagged at her how
much women in business struggled to make ends meet.
She told me that one day she read a disheartening statistic
about women-owned businesses. "Most startling to me,"
she said, "was that out of 10.5 million women-owned businesses, only 243,000 are at $1 million in revenue. I really
had to sit down and think about that because I knew there
were a million men at the $1 million mark."

So Nell decided to do something about it—in effect,
to solve the next problem. In 2005 she launched the Make
Mine a Million $ Business (M3 for short) campaign. Her
goal was ambitious: to help 1 million women entrepreneurs reach $1 million in revenues. She created a series of
competitions in large cities across the country for women
business owners whose companies had revenues of at least

$250,000. A panel of judges picked the winners, who received financing, business coaching, and other assistance that would help push them toward the $1 million goal. It was an ambitious and successful program, born from the conviction of one woman that she could be a game-changer.

What has impressed me most about Nell is that she isn't just about helping individual women succeed. She views herself as contributing to the revival of a sagging economy. When I asked her what she wants to accomplish long term, she replied, "A million women, making $1 million in revenue, 4 million new jobs, and $700 billion pumped into the economy. I know I'm going to see that. I know I am."

Vision means having the foresight to look ahead and solve the next problem. True visionaries don't rest on their laurels, nor do they rely on the obvious solutions. They're always thinking of new twists on the old themes. When Michael Pollan, bestselling author of *The Omnivore's Dilemma*, discussed his book *In Defense of Food: An Eater's Manifesto*, I thought he'd be talking about dietary choices. But his real message was about health care: "People designing the health care system don't know how essential what we eat is to the future of health care." I realized that Michael was taking a visionary approach, moving beyond the simple message of what we put on our plates to a strong, futuristic policy position.

Mike Milken, who founded the Milken Institute, had a similar vision about health care. During the national debate on health care reform, when everyone was talking about how to insure 47 million uninsured Americans and at the same time lower costs, Mike turned the issue on its head by zeroing in on obesity. "Did you know," he asked, "that an obese person will cost a company four times what a smoker will because that person has a high probability of developing diabetes and heart disease?" By Mike's reckoning, 70 percent of the money spent on health care is related to lifestyle and behavioral issues. Instead of focusing on private versus public plans, Mike looked at how each of us can take personal responsibility—evaluating exactly where we contribute to the problem. Mike's vision was to bring everyone into the discussion, to show how we each have a stake in the health care debate.

You don't have to have deep pockets to put your vision into action. Great ideas can emerge from the most ordinary places. When Fred Smith was a student at Yale University, he worked as a charter pilot flying out of the New Haven airport, which served many high-tech companies. He saw how difficult it was to meet the growing need to provide computer parts quickly. Fred made a simple but profound observation: "The world was going to automate," he related to me, "and the automated world was going to require a different type of logistics system that allowed you to supply the entire country on a nondiscriminatory basis." He wrote a term paper, detailing a business plan for a new kind of transport company. His professor wasn't impressed. He gave Fred a mediocre grade.

Fred was just a kid. He didn't have the wherewithal

to put his idea into action. But he never stopped thinking about it. After graduation, he joined the Marine Corps and served in Vietnam. Observing the military's logistical systems, he thought about how he could apply that knowledge to the company he planned to start. When he returned to civilian life, he began to put a plan into motion. In 1971, with the help of a small inheritance and a handful of investors who believed in him, he founded Federal Express. Clarity of vision laid the groundwork for everything Fred did after that.

One caveat: If you have a vision, you have to back it up with the goods. In recent decades we have been a nation that has replaced making things with making money. Creative financial "products" that generated profits, without the solid underpinning of *real* products, have been called innovative. These financial products made money for a while, until they didn't sell anymore. Then the bottom fell out. There was no *there* there. True vision translates into something solid and lasting—something tangible. Randy Jones, the founder of *Worth* magazine, recently illustrated that point to me during a discussion of his new book, *The Richest Man in Town: The Twelve Commandments of Wealth*. Randy identified the richest men (and several women) in one hundred American towns and cities, and investigated the secrets to their success. The one consistent quality he discovered was that his subjects were not goal setters, but executors. "Vision without execution is hallucination," he told me. "Execution is everything. I was surprised to find that often they did not have a master plan. They just determined every day to do something better."

Balance big dreams with reality checks

America is a country of big dreams, and the idea that bigger is better has been a guiding principle for a long time. It's so ingrained in our self-understanding that few people saw the warning signs that constant, rapid growth was unsustainable. One man who did was David M. Walker. In mid-2007, before the collapse of the financial markets, David, who was then the comptroller general of the United States, began speaking out about the dangers of wasteful government spending. His most colorful analogy was that our country was in the same situation as the Roman Empire before its fall, when relentless international acquisition and fiscal irresponsibility destroyed the solid foundation of the greatest nation in the ancient world. "With the looming retirement of baby boomers, spiraling health care costs, plummeting savings rates, and increasing reliance on foreign lenders, we face unprecedented fiscal risks," he warned. David's commonsense prognosis, delivered with a sharp edge, rubbed many people the wrong way, but his prediction just about came true during the 2008 financial crisis.

In 2008 David left government to become the president and CEO of the Peter G. Peterson Foundation, whose mission is advocacy and education to promote financial responsibility. His life's work has become helping the nation balance big dreams with reality. When I asked David about his definition of success, he told me that early on, it was all about his personal career and family, but in later years he saw that he had a broader role to play in serving the country. I asked him to name his model for success, and he replied, "Theodore Roosevelt. He overcame illness as a child to accomplish great things. He was a progressive, a fiscal conservative, an internationalist, and an environmentalist who did what he thought was right, even if it wasn't popular."

Ranjay Gulati, professor of business administration at Harvard Business School, has a valuable insight about how we tend to overplay the idea of big change when it comes to implementing a vision. "Life," he told me, "is also about making change happen, and finding that balance between big and small change and getting them to work together." Ranjay used a sports metaphor, the "small ball" theory, to illustrate his point. "In life, you hit the ball out of the park—a home run—once in a while," he said. "In the interim, you've got to survive. You've got to make things happen. So it's a question of finding the right balance between saying, 'I want to hit the ball out of the park' and 'I want to keep hitting singles and doubles as well.'" What counts is scoring runs, and if you hit enough singles and doubles, the runs start to accumulate.

In the course of a life, playing small ball matters as much as the home runs. Many people think of success as an end point. They talk about "making it." But true success is a way of being that happens every day. If you're going to stay on that long road, you need to have victories along the way to keep you motivated. If you learn to recognize the small achievements and value them as much as you do the home runs, then you will always be successful.

Embrace innovation

In 2007 I did a series for CNBC called *The Business of Innovation*. It was a great opportunity to bring together the best minds in business for lively discussions about how companies thrive. The result was a treasure trove of insight as we explored the question: Why are some companies able to transform themselves and evolve, while others sputter and die as times change? As I was doing the series, I realized that this question is fundamental, not just for companies, but also for individuals. Look around you. What is the difference in attitude between people who come back from the ashes and those who are buried by them?

One of the participants, Roger Schank, has a long history of being on the leading edge of corporate learning. He founded the acclaimed Institute for the Learning Sciences at Northwestern University and currently runs Socratic Arts, a company devoted to high-quality e-learning for businesses and schools. Roger noted that the key for companies, as well as individuals, is an understanding of the true meaning of one's work and ambitions, even as the superficial elements shift. Roger believes that tradition can be a bad thing if it becomes a rigid identity. If you say, "We're *this* kind of company" or "I'm *this* kind of person," it can limit you. Roger also believes that to be truly innovative you have to be clear about your core mission, not just its trappings. In the media business, this has become particularly clear. Ten years ago, if you had asked the head of NBC, "What do you do?" he would have replied, "We're a television broadcasting company." Today, that answer would be completely inadequate. NBC might be described as a *content* company—and the content, be it news, entertainment, sports, business, or other, can be delivered in a variety of ways.

Professor Amar Bhidé, an economist who taught business at Columbia University, believes that crisis can inspire innovation. He told me, "Crisis is often a stimulus for the adoption of new technologies. Most people don't know this, but the 1930s were the years of the highest productivity growth in the twentieth century. A lot of new technologies were developed because people were looking for an angle to improve their productivity. Another example: the computer revolution took off in the early 1980s, when we had a recession. It proved that access to the credit markets, which were dead at the time, isn't necessary for innovation. Microsoft was started without any credit. Ultimately, what makes the economy grow is innovation, the drive of innovators to develop new products and services, and the venturesomeness of consumers to use them."

When I heard him use the word "venturesomeness," I thought of a story Bill Gates Sr. told me about his son's first encounter with a computer. It was 1968. "Bill's mother and I decided to send him to the Lakeside School because, well, he seemed a little different and we weren't sure he was going to prosper in public school," Bill said. "And if we hadn't made that decision, the world of Bill Gates would have been very different. Because the Lakewood School had a computer in the basement, a big boxy thing that looked like an old teletype machine. Bill and three or four other boys [including Paul Allen] really took to it, spending hours with it and learning everything they could about the software. You could say they were addicted."

When I heard this story, I realized that on the one hand, Bill Gates's introduction to the computer was an example of luck. But the venturesomeness part was what he did with it. He took a dusty old machine and turned it into the most successful commercial venture of the technological age.

Ask yourself how you are being innovative. Where is the "venturesomeness" in your life? How are you contributing to your personal growth and the growth of the economy? How is the work you do every day making an improvement on a model that wasn't functioning so well? How do events like the recent financial crisis stimulate you to take actions you never imagined possible before?

Let the sunshine in

In June 2009 I visited the "Googleplex," the corporate headquarters of Google, located in Mountain View, California, a bedroom community of San Jose. My mission was to answer the question Why is Google so successful?

During my reporting, I interviewed many of the key players, including the CEO, Eric Schmidt. I also walked around the complex and talked to staffers in various departments. Google has a beautiful campus with a parklike outdoor seating area, a gym and volleyball court, many massage stations, and free food in all of the cafeterias. A large sculpture of a dinosaur sits in the center of the grounds—a striking reminder that those who can't innovate will perish.

Google spends lots of money on employee perks to keep its people happy. They realize that in today's world, you have to allocate time differently since technology allows work to happen 24/7. Employees might work for a few hours, get a massage or play a game of volleyball, and go back to work. Google purchased one thousand bicycles and placed them all over the campus, making it easy to ride from building to building.

Everything about the Googleplex fosters social networking, based on the philosophy that when smart people are free to interact and exchange ideas, creativity happens. There is an absence of the claustrophobic mentality that afflicts many companies, that stunts growth and discourages performance. Google lets the sunshine in. For example, the company has a concept called "20 percent time," which allows employees to do what they think is most important for one-fifth of their work time, whether it's Google-related or not. Some critics think it's an insane policy. Why would Google give away 20 percent of its productivity? In fact, Google has found that by trusting employees to experiment and enjoy the process, they are inspired to be more productive. It tells the employees that management trusts and respects their ideas. One thing is for sure: The best thing—and the most important thing—about successful companies is the people. Google makes its people feel loved and valued. This is a continuing thread throughout successful companies. Google does what Jack Welch believed and has told me many times: Reward excellence and make people feel good. They, in turn, will work harder and longer.

As I walked around the campus, I asked many of the workers why *they* thought Google was so successful. The names of the founders, Larry Page and Sergey Brin, came up a lot. Across the board, workers believed that the Google founders had so infused the company with a culture of creativity and vision that it was easy to get in the groove. "We all know and understand the vision," they said repeatedly. Employees also told me that the founders set an inspiring goal: Do no evil and change the world for the better. Don't nickel-and-dime the changes; attack the big problems. One worker recalled his tenure at another media company before coming to Google. "It was always very hard to understand what our mission was," he said. "Here the mission is clear: organize the world's information."

Eric Schmidt explained the culture of Google to me this way: "When Larry and Sergey first founded the company, they had the notion of the company as family. And what do families do? They eat together. They have fun together. And especially when you're their age, it's like a dorm atmosphere. I tend to think of Google as an extension of graduate school—similar kinds of people, similar kinds of crazy behavior, but people who are incredibly smart and incredibly motivated and have a sense of change, a sense of optimism. To work at Google is to live in an enriching environment. If you look past the food and the perks and the lava lamps, what you see is a culture where people feel they can build things, that they can actually accomplish what they want. And ultimately, people stay in companies when they see they can achieve something."

I concluded my visit convinced that Google has created a template for a new way of doing business in a technologically advanced world, one based on openness and creativity. The vision of the founders—don't be afraid of progress, be open to ideas, take the big chances—is one that I am sure will be replicated by other companies. Today Google's work environment is the envy of many. Tomorrow it may be common practice.

3

Initiative

Keep rattling the cage

In 1994 I became the first person to do televised reports from the floor of the New York Stock Exchange. The learning curve was huge, not just for me but also for the guys on the floor. Not only was I exposing their inner sanctum to the world, I was breaking into a very exclusive boys' club. They weren't all thrilled to see me there. Even though Dick Grasso, the CEO of the Exchange, was committed to the experiment, they didn't exactly roll out the red carpet. The ladies' room was in the basement.

When you're the first, there are always going to be people who question you and some who want to see you fail. That's just a fact of life. I wasn't naïve about it. But like most women who broke into male-dominated professions, I'd learned how to earn respect by working hard and being friendly and tenacious, and I fully expected that I'd be able to bring the guys around.

I had been there a couple of weeks when I met George, the specialist and market maker for GE, the parent company of CNBC. George was great. He took the time to explain to me how trading works, and he was a good teacher. I appreciated George, and I wanted to return the favor. So when I heard that Jack Welch, GE's CEO, was planning to visit the floor, I saw my chance. I'd take him and introduce him to George, and Jack could see what a fantastic job he was doing. I was also was thrilled to be able to be the one to show Jack around the Exchange floor, particularly the post of GE.

A couple of days before Jack's visit, I went over to George's post to let him know about it. As I approached, I saw that there were about twenty guys standing around, but it was quiet. It didn't look as if there was too much going on. I walked up and said quietly, "George . . ."

One of the older traders, who was standing there jotting notes on a little pad, snapped his head around at the sound of my voice. His face was full of pure rage. "Run along!" he yelled at me. "You will not come over here. You are not welcome. Don't you come here again. Run along!" He was shouting loud enough to draw attention from all of the traders in the vicinity. About twenty-five traders were within earshot, watching. I was mortified.

Run along? I was stunned. I had never been spoken to so dismissively in my professional life. For a moment I couldn't move. I'm sure my face was bright red. The crowd of guys was standing there watching me, looking for a response—waiting for a fight, even. I had knots in my stomach. Finally, I summoned every iota of dignity I could muster and replied with a shaking voice, "Do not speak to me that way." And I turned and walked away. George followed me, apologizing, and several others murmured supportively as I passed them. But this guy, who shall forever remain nameless, had thrown down the gauntlet, and I couldn't just let it go.

I called Dick Grasso. "I'm not going to stand for this," I told him.

Dick sighed. "Maria, you have to understand that there are people that do not want you here," he said. "What we are trying to do is new to all involved." He explained that some people didn't want me there not only because I was a woman, but because I was a reporter with a camera, and they didn't want their business blasted across the television screen. "That's just the way it is," Dick said. I was angry. "Look," I said, "I'll be here or I won't be here, but if I'm going to stay, I won't tolerate having people screaming at me because I'm trying to do my job."

Dick arranged a sit-down in his office with me and my new nemesis, who, it turned out, was actually on the board of the Exchange. Great. The meeting was a disaster. The guy didn't even look at me. He was clearly annoyed as hell. He finally snarled, "Look, I don't watch your little TV show, and I don't know what you think you're trying to do, but stay out of my way. Don't even think of coming near my post." And the meeting closed on that note.

It might have been no big deal. So, one trader didn't like me. Who cared? But this guy decided to be my enemy, and for several years he tried his best to make my life miserable. Every single time I passed his post, he would let loose with a string of disparaging comments, and I confess that I let him get to me. I'd meekly tiptoe by, feeling a knot in my stomach. I was scared of him. I was embarrassed. For a long time I took a detour just so I wouldn't have to pass him. And after five years of avoiding him and listening to his cutting remarks and having him gossip about me, I'd finally had enough. I started walking by with my head held high, determined to give as good as I got. One day during the dot-com sell-off, when so many people were losing money, he called after me, "Maria, you'd better save your money." In other words, "You're not going anywhere, so save it now." This time, I yelled back, "No, you'd better save *your* money." It felt like high school, but I was tired of ceding the upper hand.

Over the years things really changed on the Exchange floor. The market began to tank during the dot-com bust. Everyone was losing money, and people started losing their jobs—including my tormenter. I didn't see him again for a few years, and then coincidentally ran into him at a party. He came up to me with a friendly smile. "Maria," he said, "I know I've given you a hard time, and I'm sorry." He put out his hand for a shake, as if we were old buddies. It was a twist of fate. After so many years working at the NYSE, I had made many friends and had many allies, but this guy just would not accept me until he was gone. "No problem," I said. "Take care."

Sometimes, when you're in the public eye, people forget that you're human and that you're trying to do your job, just like everyone else. Being first on the scene requires initiative and stamina. I've never met a successful woman who didn't have a story to tell that was similar to mine. But if you're going to get anywhere, you have to learn to take the hits and rise above them. If you do a good job, the conflict will eventually disappear. Today I feel as if I belong on the floor. I've earned my place. In the process, I paved the way for the other reporters who followed me.

Taking the initiative is always a risk. You are sticking your neck out for sure. You risk being laughed at, being ridiculed, or, worse, being wrong. But if you believe in what you are doing and are trying to do the right thing in every instance, you will ultimately win.

Go get it

I'll never forget Marjorie Mandell, a journalism teacher I had at NYU. She taught feature writing, and she was young and hip—my first guide in learning how to pursue a story. She forced me to get out of myself and into the world by giving me assignments like going to the Trump Tower and writing about the comings and goings of the people there; or going to the Public Theater near the NYU campus to watch a show and then ask audience members what they thought. These simple exercises were my initiation into journalism. They also helped build my courage and taught me how to be bold and get out in front of a story.

It's clear to me that if you want to be successful, you have to imagine what you want and then go get it. You can't hang back, a lesson I also learned from Irene Rosen-feld, chairman and CEO of Kraft Foods. Irene is an incredibly accomplished woman, consistently near the top of *Fortune* magazine's "Most Powerful Women in Business." Irene told me that one of the keys to success is to ask for what you want. "Some of my most significant promotions were for jobs that I had expressed a strong desire for," she said. "But that boldness doesn't always come naturally to many women. Unfortunately, girls are not socialized to 'toot their own horns' or to ask for things. If a man wants something—say, to stop for ice cream—he'll just come out and say that he wants to get some ice cream. Many women, on the other hand, say, 'Oh, there's an ice cream shop over there,' or 'Gee, ice cream would taste good on such a hot day.' So be direct. If you want ice cream, say you want ice cream, what flavor, in a cone or a cup, and how many scoops! It may seem like a trivial example, but it plays out in so many ways."

Be first on the scene

Some of the most successful people I know have dared to step out over the edge and do something no one else had ever tried before. They saw a need and asked what they could do to address it. For Dr. Muhammad Yunus, founder of Grameen Bank, that need presented itself in the mid-1970s during the famine that ravaged his homeland of Bangladesh. At the time, Muhammad was teaching economics in the United States. "I was feeling very restless teaching elegant theories of economics while people were dying," he told me. "I knew I had to do something about it. And I wondered, why can't we do something in a business way to help solve these problems?"

Muhammad saw tremendous motivation and ingenuity in the people of Bangladesh, but their efforts to prosper were foiled by their inability to get loans. He was inspired by the plight of one woman who sold handicrafts to feed her family, but who was sinking into debt because of the predatory high-interest loan she had received from a local bank. The amount of the loan: twenty-five cents. Her debt: hundreds of times that amount.

Muhammad came up with the idea of micro loans, which were small interest-free loans for villagers to start their own businesses and become self-sustaining. When he started Grameen Bank, he had many detractors. His micro-lending program seemed to fly in the face of banking wisdom—you don't lend money to poor people who can't pay it back. But he beat the odds and revolutionized development in poverty-stricken countries. His concept worked. Today, Grameen Bank lends out half a billion dollars a year, and in 2006 Muhammad Yunus won a Nobel Peace Prize for his efforts. In 2009 President Obama awarded him the Presidential Medal of Freedom for his achievement. Muhammad says, "My dream is that someday Grameen Bank will be known as the bank of the formerly poor."

Do you have an idea that is burning in the back of your mind? Ask yourself what is stopping you from pursuing it.

The only difference between the people who are first on the scene and the people who follow them is the commitment to act.

Do the unthinkable

Every so often I meet a person whose road to success was so extraordinary that it makes me sit up and take notice. Ron Meyer, the president and COO of Universal Studios, is one. When I visited him at his home in Los Angeles, he was wearing a short-sleeved shirt and his tattoos were clearly visible. One doesn't really expect to see tattoos on such a high-powered business executive, but Ron wears them as a badge of honor—a reminder of where he started and how far he's traveled.

Ron got his first tattoo when he was only fourteen; then at fifteen he quit high school. He was a kid in trouble, a drifter who didn't have a plan. He spent his time hanging out on the streets, boxing at the gym, and playing pool. At seventeen, with few prospects, he joined the Marine Corps.

The Marine Corps changed his life, but not in the way you'd expect. During his stint, he contracted measles and was quarantined. To help him pass the time, his mother sent him a book titled *The Flesh Peddlers,* a glamorized account of the life of a talent agent. Ron was enthralled. He had found his calling.

When he got out of the service, he started pounding the pavement, going to all of the talent agencies. At each one he said, "I'll do anything you want me to do. I'll work in the mail room. I'll run errands. Anything." And in each case, he was turned away. With little education and no experience, his prospects were slim to none. But one day he got a tiny break. The Paul Kohner Agency called. Paul Kohner's driver had quit, and they needed someone immediately. Ron canceled a trip to Europe with friends and showed up the next day. The job paid $75 a week, and he turned it into gold.

Kohner represented some of the biggest stars of the day—among them John Huston, Billy Wilder, Charles Bronson, and Lana Turner. Ron told me, "Paul would have meetings in his car and talk about deals. I learned the business and got to know a lot of people." In the six years Ron drove for Kohner, he learned the nuts and bolts of the talent business. In fact, he became so knowledgeable that when he lied to the William Morris Agency and told them he was an agent, they believed him. In the early 1970s, Ron became a successful agent in his own right, representing the likes of Rob Reiner, Sally Struthers, Sylvester Stallone, and Farrah Fawcett.

In 1975, with four colleagues from William Morris, he formed Creative Artists Agency. Working eighteen-hour days and taking no pay for the first two years, they turned CAA into the hottest agency in town, representing top-of-the-line stars like Barbra Streisand, Cher, Madonna, Tom Hanks, and Tom Cruise. Today Ron is running Universal Studios. And he hasn't let success go to his head. He has remained down-to-earth and has worked hard to keep the company entrepreneurial. It's not hard to get Ron's ear. One day he's flying on a plane with Julia Roberts; the next day he's having lunch with a guy in the mail room. He is known as one of the nicest guys in the business. He is incredibly loyal. His staff has told me they'll do anything for him because he treats them with such respect.

So, what's the lesson for aspiring young people today? You might think that Ron's story could only have been possible in the 1960s—that today's competitive, cutthroat environment would make it unlikely that an inexperienced guy could go from the chauffeur's seat to the executive office. But I see Ron's story as timeless because it demonstrates the power of tenacity. You may have to knock on one hundred doors to get an answer. You may have to start at the bottom. But the qualities Ron demonstrated are still the key to success: he was driven, he believed in himself, he was willing to spend years listening and learning, and he refused to quit. Ron never allowed the Hollywood glamour to go to his head. His success came because he never tried to be someone he wasn't. I feel so privileged to be able to call Ron Meyer a friend. His life is an example of tenacity and hard work, but most of all of loyalty, courage, and integrity.

Ditch the black crepe

You hear a lot of talk about how you have to be tough as nails and have a thick skin to succeed, and that's certainly true. But ask any boss what he or she values most in employees, and chances are they will tell you attitude. As Jack Welch put it when I asked him, "The biggest thing that will trip you up is a glass-half-empty view of life. An 'Oh, we did that before and it didn't work' attitude. An 'I don't want to try that' attitude. No one wants to hang out with black-crepe people. You've got to exude positive energy." By "black-crepe people," Jack means those folks who seem to drape every situation with mourning cloth. He hates that kind of negativity, and he is the epitome of positive. He always has a bounce in his step. Enthusiasm is written all over his face. Jack has always required the same kind of enthusiasm from those who work for him.

Herb Kelleher of Southwest Airlines told me that when he was looking for the right people to build his airline, "I was mostly looking for attitude. Although we valued education and expertise and experience, we wouldn't hire someone who had those things but also had a lousy attitude. We'd take someone with lesser credentials and a positive attitude because that's what produces a strong team."

The great trick about having a positive attitude is that you can create one, whether you feel it or not. Face it, even if you're doing what you love, you're not going to wake up singing every single day. Recently I had to fly to Chicago on a Saturday afternoon to emcee a charity dinner. It happened to be a stunning, sunny day in New York, and the last thing I wanted to do was trudge out to LaGuardia Airport and get on a plane. I could feel a whine growing—

"Oh, why do I have to do this?" I was annoyed. But I had made a commitment and realized that I couldn't go into the event with a lousy frame of mind. I had to change it. And that's what I did. I talked myself into it. By the time I got to Chicago, I was all smiles. It wasn't phony—I simply made an effort to think about the positives of making the trip and pushed my negative thoughts to the background. I reminded myself how fortunate I was to have been asked to attend, and what an honor it was to represent such an important charity. These pep talks you give yourself can actually *produce* positive feelings. Cherish the opportunities that spring from having a positive frame of mind.

Play with the boys

When I interviewed Sarah Palin, I was curious about where she got her phenomenal confidence. The former governor of Alaska who was John McCain's vice presidential running mate on the 2008 Republican ticket is extremely personable and energetic. She seems unfazed by criticism. Whatever one might think of her politics, few would disagree that Sarah Palin has been successful, both personally and professionally. She'll be on the national radar for a long time to come.

I asked her, as she looked back on her life, what she attributed her success to, and she gave me a surprising answer. "It was sports," she said. "My dad and mom were both coaches. I grew up in a family where we were very active, very competitive, and where gender was never ever an issue. The girls were expected to be out there chopping wood for the woodstove, and hunting and fishing and doing all that you do in Alaska. Everyone was equal. The combination of being involved in sports and having gender never be an issue gave me an edge."

There's no question that Palin's experience is a great lesson for young girls. But it can also be applied to everyone who strives to have a place at the table. First, you have to believe that you belong there. There are many young people who may claim a disadvantage in life—by virtue of gender, race, disability, or economic circumstances. But if you internalize the belief in your own equality, the playing field is yours to conquer. Her message: Don't be a victim. Just do it, and do it well.

Don't join the entitlement culture

Entitlement chokes initiative. If you expect to get preferential treatment because of who you know, what your last name is, how you look, or any other reason apart from initiative and hard work, you can never really achieve success. You'll always be vulnerable.

This isn't an easy lesson for many people to learn. I've noticed that ever since I joined the board of trustees of New York University, I've become every parent's best friend. I get letters and e-mails from people I barely know, asking me to put in a good word for their sons, daughters, cousins, and next-door neighbors. They figure that connections grease the wheels of success. But I disagree. I don't know these kids. I can't vouch for them. I won't play the game. It's an entirely different matter if a young person takes the initiative and approaches me on his or her own. If they want to tell me what they have achieved, and describe their accomplishments and ambitions, I'm all ears. But Dad and Mom need to stay out of the process.

Entitlement is a crippling burden. The fact is, people won't respect you if they know you've had it easy. And if you're fortunate enough to have been born into privilege, know that you'll always have to work harder than everyone else to prove yourself. That's the natural balance of things.

From an early age I learned that there was a connection between what you do and what you get. There was no entitlement in my family. When I was five years old and the Mister Softee ice cream truck came down the street, I would run to my mother, begging for ice cream. "You can have it, but can you afford it?" she would say. "How much change do you have in the jar?" I saved change as a child, and the message was clear. If I had saved enough for an ice cream cone, I could have one. If not, I couldn't. That was it. No arguments. This simple lesson built a foundation for me that I've carried through my entire life. If I wanted something, I had to work for it, or save for it, or study for it, or plan for it. It was my secret for success, and it holds true to this day.

I feel sorry for the kids who don't have an opportunity to learn this lesson, who are raised to feel entitled without having to lift a finger. A couple of years ago, I was chatting with a source on Wall Street, an extremely successful and wealthy man. He was joking about his ten-year-old's expensive tastes. "He's always nagging me: 'Dad, are we flying commercial or private? Are we sitting in box seats?'" This guy was laughing about it. He almost seemed proud. I just stared at him. "Your *ten-year-old* is asking if you're flying commercial or private?" I asked, astonished.

"Yeah," he said with a chuckle. "Isn't that funny?"

I just shook my head, thinking no, it's not funny. It's disgusting. That kid is going to be damaged. Because here's the truth: Success is fleeting. Money can be lost. If you don't have a foundation of achievement and values, you'll get swept away with the tide.

Begin at the beginning

A few years ago I was looking for an assistant and a very accomplished young woman applied for the job. She blew me away with her credentials. She had an MBA and she'd worked on Wall Street. She was smart as a whip. She knew how the markets worked and understood the technical basis of Wall Street jargon. She wanted to get into television, and she was eager to make a start with me. I was impressed.

But during our interview, she started listing her demands. "I need a dedicated computer, a mobile device, a private office," she said, ticking off her requirements. "And

I need Thursdays off. And I am never available on weekends." As she went on and on, my eyes glazed over and my heart sank.

Sitting across the table from this candidate, who was growing less promising with every word, I thought, "She doesn't even know what she's saying. She has no idea of the impression she's creating." Obviously, she didn't get the job.

When I'm hiring someone, I have a very strong bias for the bootstrap types because I was one myself. Recently my mom, who is a notorious pack rat, brought me a box of my old résumé letters. I got a kick out of reading them and being reminded of the girl I was then. The text basically boiled down to the plea: "Please hire me. I'll do *anything.*" When I started my first job at CNN, I let them know that there was no job beneath me. I'd make a coffee run, stand for hours at the Xerox machine, be a messenger. I probably would have cleaned the bathrooms if they'd ask me, I was so happy to be there. I didn't expect to be handed the keys to the executive office the minute I walked in the door. I didn't mind getting my hands dirty. It worked. When people see that you're willing to do the scut work, they'll respond by giving you increasing responsibilities. No one likes a prima donna.

Actually, on second thought, I would not have cleaned the bathrooms. The point is, be flexible and open, but don't take it too far. If you want to write scripts and your boss wants you to clean bathrooms, there's clearly a gap in expectations that has to be resolved.

Get on the plane

I've made it a theme of my career that when I want something, I just do it. I make the call, I get on the plane, I go for it. It doesn't always work out, but I know I can't sit back and wait for the phone to ring.

In the late summer of 2008, my show was doing a special on the energy business and my producer suggested interviewing Sarah Palin. I was on vacation with my sister in Arizona, and I wasn't too thrilled with the idea of going all the way to Alaska. I really wanted to get home at that point. My sister, noticing my lack of enthusiasm, chastised me: "Oh, get on the plane, Maria. You're so lucky to have a chance to go to a great place like Alaska." She was right, of course, and besides, the story, as it turned out, was too important to just phone it in.

Once I arrived, I could feel that something was in the air. I conducted a lengthy interview with Governor Palin about energy, but I couldn't ignore the underlying sense that something big was going on. John McCain was scheduled to announce his running mate in a week, and Palin's name had been mentioned. At that point, no one expected him to select her, but I asked perfunctorily if she'd been contacted by the senator. As Palin glanced nervously at her PR guy and mumbled that maybe she was on a list but she didn't really know, I thought, "Hmmm." After the interview, I asked Palin if I could interview her again midweek for my *BusinessWeek* column. I wanted to keep the contact alive, just in case.

I interviewed Palin by phone on Wednesday, and she sounded very confident. Our discussion went beyond energy and into general economic issues. And again I thought, "Hmmm."

On Friday John McCain announced that he'd chosen Sarah Palin as his running mate. That Sunday my interview aired, and I was the first reporter to have a full-fledged sit-down with the new candidate. All because I took the extra step. Of course, I had no idea at the time how the story would unfold. I was lucky. But I made my own luck by getting on the plane and making the effort.

Bank goodwill for the long term

The world we live in isn't a patient place. Everyone looks for results right now. In fact, that's part of the reason we're in such a financial mess. But one of the secrets of my success is that I'm always finding ways to bank goodwill for the future. I'm constantly aware of building relationships. Journalism is all about that. Sure, I want the interview today—the pressure is on. But I force myself to be patient. At some point I know I'll get a return on my investment. I also know that getting the story is one part tenacity and one part relationship building.

I am often asked to speak to corporate groups, schools, and charitable organizations, and when my schedule permits, I always say yes. It's one way I build goodwill. Later, those people are more likely to answer my calls.

This process is also about building trust and showing

people I'm a serious journalist. Sometimes there's a feeling that reporters have their stories written before they do the interviews. It's important for me to show that I'm willing to do the groundwork and listen carefully. When I traveled to Dubai and Abu Dhabi, I took the time to meet with some leaders of the investment arm of the Abu Dhabi government. They were very suspicious of the media, but the time I spent explaining my show and what I was about went a long way in easing their concerns. Later, when I needed information about why they were investing in certain companies, they all took my calls. They trusted me.

Relationship building takes time and persistence, but it pays off in the end. Build your Rolodex with goodwill. Don't ask what others can do for you. Ask what you can do for them.

Stay on duty

In May 2006 I got caught up in a flurry of controversy involving Federal Reserve chairman Ben Bernanke, who was new to the job after Alan Greenspan's seventeen-year reign. Bernanke had just given his first testimony before Congress, and the markets rallied on his suggestion that the Fed was finished raising interest rates. I then ran into him at the White House Correspondents' Dinner, and I asked him about it.

I was standing in a small circle, which included Robert Hormats, vice chairman of Goldman Sachs, talking to Bernanke. Hormats was asking him many sensitive questions about labor costs, inflation, and the like, and Bernanke just smiled in every case and refused to answer. But my own question—"Did the markets and the media get it right by rallying after your testimony?"—he answered in depth. To my amazement, he told me that the markets would be wrong to conclude that the Fed was not going to raise rates in the future. Our conversation, though informal, was not off the record, and I figured that Bernanke would never have spoken so openly in front of Hormats if he wanted it kept under wraps. So I reported our conversation the following Monday, and the markets plunged with the news.

I took some flack for the scoop. Some people thought I'd blindsided Bernanke by reporting a conversation that took place when he was "off duty." But from my standpoint it seemed to be a perfectly open discussion. I figured that Bernanke wasn't going to give me and Hormats information that others weren't privy to. In fact, I later asked Hormats what he did with that information. "Naturally," he said, "I told my trading desk." As I would have assumed. It was one more reason it was important that I report it, because I believed everyone should have that same access to important information.

It took initiative for me to put myself in a setting where I learned important information and then not to drop the ball once it was in play.

4

Courage

Be bold, smart, and fair

My grandmother Rosalia Maria Morreale was the most courageous person I have ever known. Although she was born in the United States, Italian was her first language, and she returned to Italy when she was a child. Later, as a young married woman once more living in the United States, her experience was in some ways more like that of an immigrant than a native American. She and my grandfather settled in Brooklyn and started a family. But when my mother was only six, my grandmother was tested again with the death of my grandfather. Now she was alone with four children, two boys and two girls, still speaking very little English. Somehow she held her family together, working in a factory and never showing her children that she was afraid.

She continued to live in her house on 17th Street in Brooklyn until she died. When my mother married, she and my father lived there for a time, in an upstairs apartment. I spent my first months of life in that house before my parents moved to Bay Ridge, which was considered a better neighborhood.

When I was a little girl, my grandmother was the center of my life. She was the stable, courageous force of our family. I looked up to her and adored her. My happiest memories are of sitting in her kitchen.

In 1977, when I was ten years old and my grandmother was seventy-four, I accompanied her and my uncle's family on a trip to Florida. I was thrilled to be part of the adventure, and my grandmother promised my mother that she would watch over me. Coming back, we were anticipating a big welcome-home party at my parents' house. Driving through Delaware, we decided to stop and rest. As we pulled off the freeway, our small hatchback was slammed by a tractor trailer, and we were sucked underneath and spat out the other side. Miraculously, I survived with minor injuries, but I can still remember the sight of my grandmother's broken body lying next to the wheel of the truck. She had been thrown from the car and remained in a coma for nine weeks before she died.

My grandmother's death was devastating to our entire family. My mother, who is a religious woman, assured me that she was safe in heaven, and even though I believed it too, I felt cheated of her presence. As the years went by, I thought with regret about all the questions I would have liked to ask her. I wanted to know where she got the courage to make the long journey to America, and how she managed to be so strong when she was left a widow at a young age. But although she wasn't there in the flesh to answer my questions, I could feel her presence, as if she were an angel sitting on my shoulder, directing me and helping me make the right decisions.

To this day, whenever I feel scared or uncertain, I can hear her calm, steady voice telling me to be strong. I speak to her often. "How will we get through these changes?" I ask her, and I can feel a soothing answer from the woman who never let change and upheaval daunt her.

My grandmother taught me that courage isn't a lofty ideal. Most of us aren't called upon to be courageous in earth-shattering ways. In the ordinary challenges of life, courage is the voice that tells you to just do it.

Just do it

A couple of years ago, I was asked to throw out the first pitch at a New York Yankees game. I was excited and flattered, but I also had a knot in my stomach. My pride was at stake. New York fans are a tough crowd, and I wasn't about to be booed out of Yankee Stadium! But I'm not a baseball player, and it's a long way (sixty feet, six inches) from the pitcher's mound to home plate, and I could easily imagine the ball landing with a thud about halfway there.

I was on vacation in Arizona when I received the request, and I went to my friend Dan, who is a hiking guide and a true athlete, and asked him if he would teach me how to pitch. Every day for two weeks, Dan worked with me, and by the end I was feeling pretty good about my pitching. But then came the big day, and I woke up terrified. Who was I kidding? I didn't belong on the pitcher's mound at Yankee Stadium. This was going to be a disaster.

Dan was in town to accompany my husband and me to the game, and when he showed up, I blurted out, "Oh, God, Dan, I'm so nervous. What am I doing?"

And Dan looked me right in the eye and said firmly, "Maria, just remember one thing when you're standing on that mound. You are exactly where you're supposed to be." His words hit me with a powerful force. I relaxed and smiled. "Yeah, I am," I said, and off we went.

When the moment came for me to walk out to the mound, I started to lose my nerve. I was in front of sixty thousand screaming fans, with the wind blowing in my eyes and home plate looking a million miles away, and I thought, "Oh no, I'm not going to do it. I'm going to be booed." And then I took a deep breath and said, "You're exactly where you're supposed to be." And I threw the ball.

It sailed over the plate into the catcher's mitt, and the crowd went wild. One of the players yelled, "Get her in the game! She's so good. Get her in the game!" That was a sweet moment.

But the real point of this story is that Dan's words became my mantra. To this day, whenever I'm in a situation where I'm feeling scared or inadequate or nervous, I repeat them in my head: "You're exactly where you're supposed to be." And the thought helps me make the leap.

Live bravely

Courage is a way of being, not just one or a series of actions. One of the best examples for me is Maurice "Hank" Greenberg, the man who built AIG from a small insurance company into a global colossus. Hank once said to me that courage is the key to success, and his life story bears it out. When I talked with him about his early days, I was very moved by the human drama of his life. Most people know Hank only as the incredibly successful CEO of a powerful international company who endured a fall from grace and then started making a relentless comeback. But, as I discovered, there is a side of Hank that the world doesn't know.

Hank's father died when Hank was six years old. After his mother remarried, they lived on a farm in the small town of Liberty, New York, in the Catskill region about ninety miles northwest of New York City.

"When I was nine or ten, I used to have a trap line," he recalled. "I'd get up at four in the morning to milk the cows before I went to school. And when you're tramping in the woods and matching wits with fur-bearing animals, to see if they could outsmart you and figure out where you're placing the trap before it caught them, you learn things that you don't learn when you grow up in a sheltered situation."

Hank left home when he was seventeen to join the army. It was 1942, and like many young men, he felt called to contribute to the war effort. "I had to fudge my age because you had to be eighteen to enlist," he said. "I had a girlfriend who worked in the county clerk's office. I got a blank birth certificate and I filled it out, she stamped it, and then I had a birth certificate saying I was eighteen." And so Hank, a Jew, headed for Europe, where he was immediately thrown into the heat of the battle. He was only nineteen when he received a commission as a lieutenant.

When I asked Hank if he learned courage in the war, he said, "I don't think you learn courage. You either have it or you don't. You've got to overcome a lot of inner resistance in the beginning. I'd be stupid to say I never had fear. The more I saw, the more I knew that the worst could happen to me. It wasn't always going to happen to somebody else. Fear is not something that you should be ashamed of, but you have to learn to overcome it. And once you do, it's much easier. But you have to work at it. You have to grit your teeth and do what you need to do. And if you're leading men, you have to realize that they won't follow someone who doesn't appear to have not just courage but also confidence. You can't ask people to do what you won't do."

On D-Day, in June of 1944, Hank was on Omaha Beach during the invasion of Normandy. He had already been tested many times by that point, but Omaha Beach was the "Ground Zero" of the war. More than 2,200 American soldiers died there, advancing on the beach straight into enemy fire. Hank watched from a ship, waiting for the order to hit the beach. "There were ships all around us," he remembered, "and we were all worried, obviously. But

I was very lucky. My battalion commander saw what was happening on the beach we were supposed to land on, and he told the coxswain to take us down the beach by one hundred yards or so. Had he not done that, I probably wouldn't be talking to you. It was a grim experience."

In April 1945, Hank, with the Forty-fifth Infantry Division, participated in the liberation of Dachau. They were greeted with a sight of unimaginable carnage. Bodies were crammed into railroad cars and piled everywhere. Thousands of prisoners, still alive, appeared to be mere skeletons. For Hank, a young Jewish man, the scene was imprinted on his mind for life. Walking into Dachau was his last act of courage of the war. He was awarded the Bronze Star for his service.

Hank returned to the United States to find that the adjustment to civilian life was harder than the experience of war itself. He felt out of place and alone. In battle, he had been an adult, a commander. In civilian life, he was still a high-school student, since he'd skipped his senior year to join the army. "I was not going to go back to Liberty, New York, and go to high school," he said. "I was twenty years old. So I went to the Rhodes School in New York. I had a room down on West 10th Street for about five bucks a week. I finished school in about seven months. But that was the toughest time in my life. I felt so out of place. I was living alone in this goddamn walk-up, I didn't know anybody in the city, and I didn't have much money, except for the money I'd saved in the service. I was very lonely. I had spent my formative years in the military."

In spite of the difficulty, Hank was determined to finish what he'd started. He went on to college, receiving a bachelor's degree in pre-law from the University of Miami before entering the New York University law school. He graduated from law school in 1950. Hank had just finished his last classes and was driving upstate to see his mother when the news came over the radio that North Korea had invaded South Korea. Being a reservist, he was called up and shipped to Korea as a captain. "Korea was a very tough war," he said, citing the inhuman conditions that were experienced by the soldiers. "The winter I was there was just horrible. We didn't have winter clothes. I used to stuff newspapers in my boots to keep my feet warm. It was an ugly war. But you do what you have to do. And I commanded a company with about two hundred and fifty men, and then came back and had to find a job.

"It was kind of serendipity. The day after I came home, I went to visit some of the guys I went to law school with, and they were practicing negligence law in downtown New York, in the insurance district. But I didn't want to be a part of that. As I left their office and was walking down the street, I passed the insurance company Continental Casualty Company and, by accident, just walked in, and I got a job on the spot as a junior underwriter. I didn't know what the hell that meant, but I got a job. And I thought I would do that temporarily until I decided if I was going to practice law. I'm still in the insurance business."

In his new field, Hank found that he had other battles to wage. "To begin with, when I got into insurance, it was a white-shoe business—that is, the firms were run by what were called the WASP elite. Being Jewish wasn't exactly the right background to have. I had to overcome that adversity. Most of the people of the Jewish faith were either agents or brokers. They were not running insurance companies. I did not want to be an agent or a broker. That didn't appeal to me. I had a vision of building an insurance company that I thought would be different than all others, and I was determined to do it."

For a man who had fought against Hitler's army and participated in the liberation of Dachau, the brush with anti-Semitism at home was a bitter pill. "But when I was facing the barrier of being Jewish, I never once worried that I wouldn't make it. I didn't sit around and wallow in misery. That's not me. I kept doing what I thought was the right thing to do. You win people over by what you do. If you're doing it right, they begin to appreciate you. That's how you overcome the obstacles. Hank eventually became the second CEO of AIG, replacing C. V. Starr, the company's founder, in 1968.

"In business," he said thoughtfully, "courage is doing things that others have not done, and being willing to bet your own worth and take a risk because you have confidence that what you're doing is going to work out all right. I've been in the risk business—insurance—for my entire career. And I went forward and did things others had not done, such as opening new markets and going where others had not gone. I went to Russia before anybody else even thought of it, before the Iron Curtain came down. I went to China in 1975. Nobody else was even considering doing an insurance business in China then.

"Along with courage, though, you've got to have common sense. Courage isn't being reckless. It's acting on instinct, but knowledgeable instinct, and then having the energy to do what has to be done. You can have great instincts in some things, but in things which count, where somebody's life may be at stake, you've got to think it through. And in business, if you're going to make a move that could potentially damage your company severely if things don't go as expected, you've got to carefully think it through. Once you've done that, you can act decisively."

But perhaps most important, Hank emphasizes that courage requires integrity. "I don't care whether it's war or peace," he said, "you can't tell people things you don't believe yourself. You can't bullshit people into doing things that are not going to work."

Thinking about Hank's story, I marveled that he was as driven and bullish at eighty-four as he was when he was a young man. I've never met anyone quite like him. It's fair to say that most people would have been undone or at least daunted by the disastrous plunge of AIG, but Hank has steel in his eyes when he says, "Don't count me out."

Overcome the fear of failure

It doesn't take a major catastrophe such as the recent financial meltdown to cripple people with fear. I know one thing, though: When your thinking and actions are fear-based, you might as well turn off the lights and go home. A friend told me, "I watch CNBC with the sound off. I look at the arrows going up and down, and my stomach lurches. It doesn't seem real. It's like the Wizard of Oz is pulling the levers behind the screen." Many people shared similar sentiments with me during the peak of the financial crisis. Even savvy investors were talking about putting their money in what would be the equivalent of "under the mattress." While these concerns were justified, fear-based thinking had a self-fulfilling effect on the stock market. Overcoming fear was the first step to a recovery.

The personal arena is no different. Fear-based thinking is a stumbling block to success. Courage is the ability to act through the fear, in the same way that an athlete makes a risky shot—not because success is certain but because it is possible.

Stephen Pagliuca, the managing director of Bain Capital Partners and a co-owner of the Boston Celtics, is not only a very savvy businessman but also an interesting person. When I asked him how he would advise people who are struggling in these gut-clenching times, he gave me a script he wrote for a sports radio network series on sports, leadership, and life. Steve wrote that he has never forgotten a moment during a critical basketball game with his high school's archrival. It was double overtime, and Steve stepped to the line to shoot a free throw. He remembers thinking, in the melodramatic way of a teenager, that not only the game but his entire future was resting on that shot. He decided to do something daring—to take an unconventional jump shot from the line. "I thought if I missed, at least I would miss with all guns blazing," he writes. He made the shot, and the ball went in the basket. It was an exhilarating instant of triumph—before the other team came back and won the game.

Steve doesn't really remember the ultimate loss. He remembers the successful shot. "The experience proved that overcoming the fear of failure by taking a chance is critical in a moment of crisis. That crazy jump shot in the packed gym has been imprinted on my brain forever, and still helps me focus when critical situations arise in the business world today."

I would take Steve's insight one step further. Being courageous is not just about being unafraid when you face a crisis. It is also about having the inner clarity to understand the value of the crisis. Jeff Immelt, the chairman and CEO of General Electric, has faced some harrowing times since he took the reins from Jack Welch in 2001. But what he has consistently said is that the company's setbacks are not just bad news: they're lessons. When I interviewed Jeff in front of an audience at the NYU Stern School of Business, in the midst of the financial crisis of 2008, he said, "I've already seen twenty things I never thought I'd see in a lifetime, and I've already done ten things I never thought I'd have to do. And I've got the next ten lined up."

Jeff believes that operating during very tough times

can be an opportunity to push the reset button. "It is impossible to explain to people how tough it was to lead GE in September 2008, when Lehman declared bankruptcy, the government saved AIG, and there was one crisis after another," he said when we talked about it. "But," he added, "if it weren't for the crisis there would never have been the reset—the course correction that enabled us to move in a positive direction."

Over the years, as I've watched Jeff in action—sometimes taking public hits and other times demonstrating true leadership—I've been impressed by his steadiness. Jeff understands that in the human arena where the game of life is played, you're going to be thrown curveballs, and it's not the ball itself that's important, it's the way you catch it.

Give it a shot

Ron Insana, my colleague at CNBC, has a lot to say on the subject of following your heart and taking risks. Ron's story is inspiring, not only because of his achievements but also because he took a big chance, fell on his face, and came away with an incredible storehouse of wisdom and knowledge.

Ron began his broadcast career in 1984 at the Financial News Network, and continued on after it merged with CNBC. Over the course of twenty-two years he became a familiar face, reporting the biggest financial stories of the day. He was extremely popular, not only for his knowledge but also for his straightforward style, which viewers learned to trust. Ron could probably have stayed at the network and continued as a top reporter for the rest of his career, but he felt a different path calling to him. In 2006, when his contract was up for renewal, Ron took a big leap and left CNBC to do something completely different by starting a hedge fund. "I wanted a new challenge," Ron told me. "I wasn't bored. But by the time 2006 rolled around, I had accomplished everything I wanted to do in broadcast journalism. I was forty-five years old, and I just wasn't certain that I fit in anymore. The opinion business, as opposed to the news business, was becoming predominant. So I thought it was a good time to reassess.

"I had long been curious about the hedge fund business. Every superior hedge fund manager had a flow of information that was better than what I had as a journalist. I felt I was equipped to start my own company. I had been paid to get both an MBA and a Ph.D. in business economics and accumulated a great store of knowledge. I wanted to see if I could apply it in the real world of finance."

Ron left CNBC and started Insana Capital Partners. It was a big risk, but he went about the process with great care. "It didn't make sense for me to start a hedge fund immediately because I didn't have the trading experience," he said. "It was better to pick phenomenal managers to help me run the fund. So in March 2006 I went out and started hiring people. It took a year to put together. I was not afraid of taking a chance. It was an easy decision and it felt right. My wife, Melinda, gave me support. I wasn't putting my family's future at risk. Some people are 'all or nothing' types. They bet the ranch. My father tried a business endeavor and he lost money that would have allowed us to purchase a house, and we were paying rent instead of building equity. He used the house money to go out on his own, and it was a big mistake. So I knew that, had experienced it, and wouldn't put my family's well-being at stake. Still, starting a business is an extremely high-risk endeavor—not just financially but also professionally. You have to decide if you're ready to be on your own."

Ron may have done everything right, but the timing couldn't have been worse. Barely a year into his new business, the financial crisis hit Wall Street. In August 2008 Insana Capital Partners ceased doing business. In 2009 Ron returned to CNBC as a part-time analyst.

I was curious to know how Ron felt about the experience—whether he regretted his bold move. He assured me that he has no regrets. Rather, he is amazed at how much he has learned, how much wisdom he has developed to put to use in the future. He doesn't view his decision as a mistake—far from it. "The best advice I can give someone who wants to take a chance on something different is to rely on your gut. The one thing that's never failed me is listening to my gut. Then, you have to be a scrupulous planner. You can't do it without planning and doing your homework. You have to put people around you who are smarter than you, people you can trust. You don't just walk out the door and start something new. But in the end, you're taking a chance and anything can happen. I could have been the [Olympic champion swimmer] Michael Phelps of money management, but when the tsunami hit I still would have drowned. That's life.

"I don't believe having a business not succeed as planned equals failure," Ron said. "I think everything you do gives you an education. I gave it my best shot. If you don't change and grow in every avenue of your life, you run into a dead end. It's bad for your health and your happiness—win, lose, or draw. It's dangerous to get complacent, and it's easy to do if you are in the same area your whole life. If you don't follow your heart and do what you love, you won't get anywhere."

Fight for yourself

It takes courage to carve out personal space in the midst of a demanding career. Shelly Lazarus, the CEO of Ogilvy & Mather, is a tremendous success story. She worked her way up the ranks for more than thirty years, wearing different hats in the company. And like many women, she had to balance her priorities, be fully present to her job and also fully present to her children. That took courage, especially, as Shelly told me, "For a long time I was always the only woman in the room dealing with men. And I never allowed it to hold me back from what I wanted to do.

"One day my boss said to me, 'We need you at this meeting at two o'clock, Friday.' And I said, 'I can't be at that meeting because I have my son's soccer game.' He was insistent, horrified at my response. He kept saying, 'No, no, no, you have to be there.' And I told him, 'I'm sorry. In ten years people are not going to remember who was at that meeting. But in ten years my son will remember if I was at this championship that he's been preparing for a long time. I promised I would be there, and I'm going. So you're going to have to deal with me leaving at one-thirty, because that's what I'm going to do.' I missed the meeting, and they gave me a report later, and the world went on."

Personal life intersects with professional life every day. There are those who will tell you that you can't have both—and that you don't have a right to have both. But as Shelly learned, taking a stand for yourself makes you stronger, and chances are it won't kill you.

Dare to be different

A friend who is a very successful international businessman was frustrated because his college-age son was not doing well in school and just kept sucking money from his father. Finally my friend got fed up and told his son, "I'm kicking you out. You're going to China."

His son was horrified. "China?" he wailed. "What am I going to do in China?"

"I don't know," my friend replied. "I guess you'll find out. I'll get you an apartment in Beijing, and then you're on your own. Call me when you figure it out."

It was a brave and smart move. He knew his son was bright, but he also realized that he didn't fit well in the typical mode of college student. Instead of continuing to force him into a box that he clearly didn't fit, he took a gamble. It paid off. His son thrived in China. He became worldly. He matured. His father's wise move changed his life.

Bill Gates is perhaps one of the best examples of someone taking a different path than the norm. During his junior year at Harvard, he told his parents that he was taking a semester off to help run Microsoft, the little software company in Albuquerque he'd started with his childhood friend Paul Allen. "It was a blow," Bill Sr. told me, but Bill's folks figured a semester off wouldn't hurt their son.

Bill returned to Harvard after the semester, but within months Paul Allen was urgently summoning him back. "Dad and Mom," Bill said to his parents, "I need to go to back to Albuquerque again. I'll come back to Harvard, but right now I'm needed at the company."

His dad, recalling that difficult announcement, said, "Our apprehension grew by several magnitudes at that point. We were traditionalists. We had the idea that we were raising kids who would graduate from college, and it was disturbing that this one, apparently, was not going to graduate from college. Incidentally, there wasn't a darn thing we could do it about it."

In 2008, thirty-five years after he dropped out of Harvard, Bill Gates returned to deliver the commencement address and accept an honorary doctorate. "Dad, I always told you I'd come back to get my degree," he said. He just took a more circuitous route than most.

Let me be clear: The point is not to drop out of college! The point is that the conventional path is not always the best path. If it doesn't work for you, look for ways of expanding your options and trying a different route. It may be longer and end up at a different destination than you expect. But the journey itself is part of the pleasure and the achievement.

Carry a bazooka

In the fall of 2008, Treasury Secretary Hank Paulson appeared before Congress to make the biggest pitch of his life. He asked Congress to commit extraordinary sums of money to bail out the teetering financial system. Paulson called it "carrying a bazooka," an image that stuck with me. He said, "If you're walking around with a water gun in your pocket and nobody sees it, they may think you really don't have the wherewithal to do anything. But if you're walking around with a bazooka on your shoulder, everybody knows you've got the bazooka there and if you need it, you're going to use it."

I love the bazooka image. It's about having confidence and standing tall. A confident attitude inspires confidence in others. It will get your foot in the door. In a sense, boldness is the American way. No one ever tells young people, "Work hard and you'll break even." Or "Strive to reach an even keel." We're bazooka people!

One of the people I regularly talk to for insight about the financial system made an interesting observation about the stability of the system. She asked me, "What's wrong with a boom-bust economy?"

Her question took me by surprise. "A boom-bust economy is unstable," I replied. "It creates situations like the one we're in today."

She shrugged. "For me, boom and bust means opportunity," she said. "Boom and bust means access to wealth. Boom times are great, but things don't go up forever. The bust allows people to get into the market at great prices. It's a process that opens the doors. If there were only boom times, or if we had a flat-line economy, there would be no new wealth creation." She changed the way I think about a boom-bust economy.

Thomas Friedman, the notable *New York Times* columnist and author *(The World Is Flat* and *Hot, Flat, and Crowded)*, voiced a similar perspective on my show, *The Wall Street Journal Report*. "The way I look at it," Tom said, "in the nineteenth century there was a boom, a bubble, and a bust of railroads. But in the end what it left us with was a country knitted together with a wonderful railroad system. The dot-com boom, bubble, and bust left us with a wonderful Internet structure. The question is what this current financial boom, bubble, and bust will leave us with."

It's difficult at this point to see an upside to the financial crisis, but this perspective, based on taking a long view of history, is bold and hopeful. It calls upon us to live large—to view even our greatest failures as the seeds of our success.

Take risks, but watch your tail

Being courageous means that you're willing to take risks, but you have to do it with the knowledge that your decisions are going to affect others besides you. A wise friend of mine once advised, "If you're going to take risks, you have to watch your tail." He explained: "Think of yourself as a dinosaur with a long heavy tail. When you're walking around, be aware of who you're smacking with that tail." That seems like good advice, although belatedly, for the CEOs of the financial services companies. They took on tremendous risk, but they didn't look at who would be impacted if things went awry.

Reflecting on the collapse of the financial markets, Nouriel Roubini put it to me quite directly. "There was greed and arrogance on Wall Street," he said, "and nobody was listening to the risk managers. The risk *takers* had the upper hand. They created a system of freak finance, where financial development didn't help economic growth."

This lesson applies on a personal level. Get in the habit of checking the consequences of your choices and actions, and it will become second nature to watch your tail. Do it early in your career, and you'll keep doing it when you're big. Right now, your tail might not be dinosaur-sized. It might only reach the people closest to you. But as your circle widens and your influence expands, the simple rules of generosity and empathy will position you to be successful, fair, and kind.

5

Integrity

Do the right thing

What does it mean to have integrity? These days the media is full of examples of people operating without integrity. In 2008, when the financial system teetered on the brink, you might have said that the system itself lacked integrity. It had functioned for years with some flawed principles, exemplified by forty-to-one leveraging and unrealistic expectations for continually rising housing prices. A similar example is the dot-com boom of the 1990s, when investors were pouring money into companies because they had a ".com" attached to them. On CNBC we used to have a segment called "annoying little comparisons," when my colleague David Faber would look at the market values of various companies, such as JoeSchmo'sPizzaPlace.com versus Ford Motor Company. Ford's business and valuation were based on real profits and cash flow, while JoeSchmo'sPizzaPlace.com had little revenue and earnings. Yet based on the number of "hits," the dot-com would have a higher market cap than Ford. These practices lacked real integrity. They were put in place by human beings who in many cases let things slide and lost sight of their core values.

How do you keep your core values front and center, no matter what is happening around you? One way is to look for guidance from people who are models of morality. One of the best gifts my husband's father, Saul Steinberg, ever gave us was two silver-framed copies of Ben Franklin's ode to moral living. Saul engraved one for me and one for Jono, and we keep them on each side of our bed. Franklin set out to discover how to live a life of virtue— not in the abstract, but in the practical matters that confronted him. He chose thirteen virtues and committed to master them one by one. They are elegant in their simplicity, and they pretty much cover every eventuality. Most important, each one of them can be adapted to modern life:

TEMPERANCE. Eat not to dullness; drink not to
    elevation.
SILENCE. Speak not but what may benefit others
    or yourself; avoid trifling conversation.
ORDER. Let all your things have their places; let
    each part of your business have its time.
RESOLUTION. Resolve to perform what you
    ought; perform without fail what you resolve.
FRUGALITY. Make no expense but to do good to
    others or yourself; i.e., waste nothing.

INDUSTRY. Lose no time; be always employed in something useful; cut off all unnecessary actions.

SINCERITY. Use no hurtful deceit; think innocently and justly; and, if you speak, speak accordingly.

JUSTICE. Wrong none by doing injuries, or omitting the benefits that are your duty.

MODERATION. Avoid extremes; forbear resenting injuries so much as you think they deserve.

CLEANLINESS. Tolerate no uncleanliness in body, clothes, or habitation.

TRANQUILLITY. Be not disturbed at trifles, or at accidents common or unavoidable.

CHASTITY. Rarely use venery but for health or offspring, never to dullness, weakness, or the injury of your own or another's peace or reputation.

HUMILITY. Imitate Jesus and Socrates.

Ben Franklin took his virtue project seriously. These were not abstractions to him. As he wrote, "I made a little book, in which I allotted a page for each of the virtues. I ruled each page with red ink, so as to have seven columns, one for each day of the week, marking each column with a letter for the day. I crossed these columns with thirteen red lines, marking the beginning of each line with the first letter of one of the virtues, on which line, and in its proper column, I might mark, by a little black spot, every fault I found upon examination to have been committed respecting that virtue upon that day." He called it developing the *habit* of virtue. The point is, living a life of integrity doesn't just happen automatically. It must be practiced consciously and consistently.

Create a personal honor system

Integrity isn't just about not doing wrong. It's about doing the right thing: How you take care of your people. What you give back to the community. The example you set by how you live your life and how you live in an organization.

Integrity doesn't necessarily protect you from failure, but it gives you the upper hand. People are attracted to integrity and want to work alongside those they trust.

Integrity is a natural instinct. When you are at that fork in the road, at that critical instant when you have to make a choice, you'll know in your heart what's right.

I have interviewed many business and government leaders over the years, and I always remember those whose personal honor systems are more than just a sideline. In my opinion, these are the quiet heroes of business. For example, I have been impressed with Vanguard founder Jack Bogle's constant dedication to finding investing tools for the average investor. His creation of the index fund was aimed at providing better tools for investors, at better prices and greater value.

Charles Schwab's guiding principle during his entire business career has been honesty. "Clients will pay you money even when things are bad, as long as you tell them the truth," he told me. It's something he has always believed, a lesson in integrity he learned at his father's knee. When he was young, Chuck aspired to be successful in business, and of course he also wanted to make a lot of money. But from the start he found it a challenge to maintain his principles and do his job. After he graduated from business school, he got a job as a financial analyst, and he'd been working only a year when the nation experienced the stock market crash of 1962. Chuck hated seeing his firm's clients suffer, and he wanted to help them. He said to his boss, "All of our customers have lost a lot of money in this crash. We ought to be sympathetic to their positions. We ought not to charge these people for this quarter."

As Chuck remembers it, his boss was silent for about thirty seconds, and then he said, "You're fired."

Married and with a young child at home, Chuck couldn't afford to be unemployed. "I came back the next day, tail between my legs, and said, 'Look, I really need this job.'"

His boss rehired him, but Chuck continued to struggle to reconcile the conflict between doing what was good for business and doing what was right for the customer. For him, the ultimate test was whether an offering was something he would have his parents invest in. He started his own discount brokerage in 1974, with money invested by family and friends, and set out to create a company based on his principles.

I've interviewed Chuck on several occasions, and I've been impressed to see that he has never wavered from his core philosophy. When I spoke with him in 2009, in the midst of the market collapse, he once again emphasized that his number one priority was taking care of the real human beings who rely on his company. "The investor has had a lost decade," he admitted, "but we've got to be thinking about how we can give the investor a better opportunity in the next decade. That's my personal commitment."

What makes Chuck trustworthy, even in troubled times, is the evidence accumulated from a lifetime of integrity.

One positive outcome of the crisis in the financial sector is that we've opened up a national conversation about what it means to have integrity in business. That conversation has taken hold in the schools, where the future leaders of business and industry are trained—and in some cases lured to lucrative jobs. Now their motivations are changing, broadened to include an array of options that may or may not include a high salary. In the spring of 2009 a group of MBA students at Harvard created The MBA Oath, a voluntary pledge for graduating students. The pledge lays out the key tenets of professional and personal integrity:

> ↪ I will act with utmost integrity and pursue my work in an ethical manner.

↪ I will safeguard the interests of my shareholders, co-workers, customers, and the society in which we operate.

↪ I will manage my enterprise in good faith, guarding against decisions and behavior that advance my own narrow ambitions but harm the enterprise and the societies it serves.

↪ I will understand and uphold, both in letter and in spirit, the laws and contracts governing my own conduct and that of my enterprise.

↪ I will take responsibility for my actions, and I will represent the performance and risks of my enterprise accurately and honestly.

↪ I will develop both myself and other managers under my supervision so that the profession continues to grow and contribute to the well-being of society.

↪ I will strive to create sustainable economic, social, and environmental prosperity worldwide.

↪ I will be accountable to my peers and they will be accountable to me for living by this oath.

Signing the pledge is more than just paying lip service to a set of ethics. It can have the effect of making the new generation of leaders accountable to a code of behavior that can change the way business is done.

Conduct a self-vetting

Every time there is a congressional hearing for a cabinet post or a court appointment, we see how rigorous the vetting is. Each corner of a candidate's life is open to investigation. Did they pay their taxes? Did they declare their nannies? Did they pay their parking tickets? Did they accept business gifts? Did they make a careless comment about a sensitive issue? Did they get a special deal on a home or car purchase? Did they give a friend a job? Did they ever get fired? Did they pad their résumé? Did they ever have too much to drink? Did they ever lose their tempers and say something they shouldn't have? Did a brother or sister or friend do anything embarrassing?

The scrutiny is brutal, and most of us can feel a sense of relief that we don't have to undergo that level of examination in front of the world. But it is a worthwhile exercise to consider your own life and to measure your integrity. If you were to do a self-vetting, what would you find? Look in your closet and expose the skeletons. Make a list, for your eyes only. The focus should go beyond legalities, such as whether or not you paid your taxes. Consider, too, everyday ethics and behavior. We tend to put a lot of focus on the big issues, but the small moments can be the most revealing. For example, what would you say about a person who performs brilliantly in business, yet forwards a racist or sexist e-mail cartoon to friends? Or a coworker who takes credit for work that isn't his or her own? We are all tested daily by life's mundane challenges, and none of us is perfect. But if we can acknowledge our errors, we can also find ways of not repeating them.

Don't be a white knight with dirty hands

It's striking how often in public life we see examples of the most self-righteous, judgmental people getting caught in the worst scandals. Eliot Spitzer, for example, made headlines for having trysts with a prostitute. But his public upset was spotlighted mostly because of the way he presented himself as New York's attorney general—as the squeaky-clean official who refused to tolerate even the merest hint of impropriety. He was heavy-handed, and some would say not always fair, in the way he went after the big fish, like Hank Greenberg of AIG and Dick Grasso, the CEO of the New York Stock Exchange. Spitzer acted like an avenging angel: judge, jury, and executioner. He seemed to want to humiliate Greenberg, Grasso, and others he targeted. He didn't make many friends, but he didn't care. It was all black and white for him—until he got snared in the enormous sex scandal that blew up his career.

Back when Spitzer was going after the likes of Hank Greenberg, I ran into John Whitehead and his wife at a party. John, then seventy-three, was the chairman of the Lower Manhattan Development Corporation, and he had long been involved in community activities. (He is now chairman of the World Trade Center Memorial Foundation.) John had recently written an op-ed column for the

Wall Street Journal, defending Hank Greenberg against Spitzer's aggressive pursuit. His complaint was that Spitzer had essentially tried and convicted Hank in the press before a single charge was filed. John felt that was wrong. I had also been disturbed that Spitzer publicly used the word "fraud" when he referred to Hank, although we had seen no evidence of fraud. It seemed reckless because once you say it, the public perception gets formed and it's very hard to undo the damage.

At the party, John drew me aside. We talked about some of the reverberations he faced after his op-ed ran. He told me he got a call from Spitzer himself. John was so shocked that he wrote down what Spitzer said. Spitzer was in a rage, screaming on the phone. He said this was war, and that Whitehead had fired the first shot. Spitzer said he would get back at Whitehead and would make him wish he'd never written the op-ed.

I could see how rattled John was by this experience. I felt angry on his behalf, and I discussed it on the air. Eventually John told the story himself in print. Others came forward with their own stories of being bullied by Spitzer.

When Eliot Spitzer's secret life with prostitutes was exposed, everyone's first response was utter disbelief. How could such a squeaky-clean guy get himself into such a mess? He'd managed his subterfuge for years without a hint of scandal.

Still, as awful as the revelations about Spitzer's private life were, he might have had an easier time had he not spent his career as a ruthless avenging angel. When he fell, it seemed that no one rushed to lift him up or to speak in his defense. I wonder if by setting himself up as a white knight, and destroying so many lives in the process, he forfeited his own chance at redemption.

The pollster John Zogby made this point with great insight in a piece for *The Huffington Post* after the debacle. "Spitzer never suffered the foibles of those who got caught in his crosshairs," he wrote. "Once he decided on his targets, he preyed upon them and never relented. . . . Spitzer was not in any position to beg forgiveness because he never, ever forgave."

Ken Langone, a former director of the NYSE who had been a target in Spitzer's investigation of Dick Grasso, felt that Spitzer deserved judgment because he was a hypocrite. Langone told CNBC: "He destroyed reputations of people who had good reputations and deserved reputations. What he's done to people—not me, I'm standing, thank God—but the number of people whose reputations were earned that he soiled is horrible. We all have our own private hells. I hope his is hotter than anybody else's."

Get what you deserve

As a kid growing up around my father's restaurant, I received a pretty basic understanding of earnings and worth. There was a straightforward connection between what my father delivered and what he earned. He cooked his heart out to serve the best food, and he built his reputation on providing a satisfying, affordable dining experience. The day's cash receipts were a judgment on how well he had accomplished that goal. It was instant accountability: Do well, and you'll be rewarded. Do poorly, and you won't.

I think many of us were raised with a fundamental understanding that what we earn is connected to how we perform, and that's why the controversy over executive compensation has been so heated. When hardworking people, whose compensation is directly linked to their performance on the job, hear about executives in failing companies walking away with tens of millions in bonuses, it's understandable that they react negatively—especially when those companies are being propped up by taxpayers. "In real life," one of my viewers noted, "you don't get a bonus for running your firm into the ground."

As a general philosophy, I am not in favor of the government putting caps on executive pay. I don't think this should be the job of government. I believe in free markets. However, the dispute about executive compensation is a healthy check on the integrity of the financial system and a call to accountability for all business leaders.

Nell Minow, the editor and cofounder of The Corporate Library, an independent firm respected for its research on corporate governance and compensation, gave me a colorful description of the psychology of compensation, and how it has grown to such outlandish levels. Nell explained that there's a cultural element to the rise in executive pay. "I always say that investment bankers are the geishas of the financial world because they sit next to the CEO and laugh at his jokes and talk about what a big strong man he is and wouldn't it be fun to buy something together," she said. "And so CEOs looked at the investment bankers and said to themselves, 'This guy's making more than I am. I am a titan. I'm the CEO of a great big company. I'm responsible for all these employees and customers, and all this guy does is move numbers around. I should be paid as much as he is.'" This cycle of envy, according to Nell, ratcheted up the sums CEOs felt they deserved, and it was supported by the cozy relationship CEOs typically have with their boards of directors, including those who serve on compensation committees.

America is the land of opportunity, but we chafe when people view it as an opportunity to take the money and run. How can we tell children to strive for excellence when they see the lavish rewards being paid to the mediocre titans of distressed companies? What is compensation if not an acknowledgment of ability and achievement? Does crime (if only the crime of myopic thinking and flawed operations) pay? Is greed good? Surely not. What lessons can we take from the debate about compensation?

We have a tendency to tar every financial executive with the same brush of blame, and that's wrong. I know a guy who used to work at AIG, and he got a bonus of $3,000. But his name was on the bonus list, and so he looked out his window one day and saw picketers and camera crews on his front lawn. He and his family were prisoners in their home for days. He didn't deserve to be made a poster boy for corporate greed, but what happened to him is evidence of the depth of public anger.

I've never heard anyone complain that they were making too much money. But many of the decisions made by those in the financial sector—in particular, subprime mortgages—feathered the nests of the deal makers at the expense of others. When the lights go off and you are alone with your conscience, integrity requires an honest accounting. And perhaps an act of atonement, in the form of generosity.

I was impressed to read about the way one executive handled a mini-windfall he had received. Jack Windolf, the CEO of Bollinger Insurance, was paid $500,000 in deferred compensation when he sold 51 percent of his company in 2008. He took the money and wrote a check for $1,000 to each of his 434 employees. He called it a mini-stimulus package, and also said he believed it was a fair way to disburse the money. The news of Jack Windolf's gesture was a feel-good story for a few days when it hit the press. Why did it feel good? Because we all recognize and appreciate it when someone does the right thing.

Tell the truth

Like all children, when I was young it was hammered into me by my parents and by the nuns at my Catholic school to never tell a lie. Then, lies were small-time kids' stuff, usually involving whether I had finished my homework or done my chores. They were, in the vernacular of the Catholic Church, *venial* sins.

Some people think that always telling the truth is a great policy for children, but that the complexities of adult life allow for a more nuanced reading. Or, as someone once said, "Honesty is the best policy until something better comes along."

I was a bit taken aback when Alan Greenspan admitted to me, quite candidly, that he was often in the business of obfuscation when answering questions before Congress. He called it Fed-speak. "It's a language of purposeful obfuscation to avoid certain questions coming up, which you know you can't answer," he told me. "When a congressman asks me a question and I don't want to say 'No comment' or 'I won't answer,' I proceed with four or five sentences which get increasingly obscure. The congressman thinks I answered the question and goes on to the next one."

Greenspan's method might be described as clever volleying—a helpful skill in a political environment. It puts the onus on the listener to probe deeper. In Greenspan's case, it was somewhat necessary to be vague because everything he uttered, as chairman of arguably the most important institution of the world, could set off market activity.

But for most people, shading the truth is never a good business practice, and it's a slippery slope. No one can lie forever—to themselves or others. I was around when Enron managed to convince everyone that it was strong. It hid billions of dollars of debt and came out smelling like a rose, even as it was sinking. It was a carefully crafted lie, but eventually it became unsustainable. The truth came out, and Enron's leaders were convicted of massive securities fraud. Ken Lay was facing twenty to thirty years in jail when he died suddenly of a heart attack. Jeffrey Skilling was sentenced to twenty-four years in jail. Many people will say that cash flow doesn't lie; so if you are looking for cracks in any particular story, make sure to look at cash flow, not just earnings, which can be manipulated, and revenue. Cash flow will tell the truth about a company's health.

Follow your gut when you are considering working for a company, in terms of integrity. Join companies that are based on honesty, work for people who encourage open communication and dissent, and remember that even the small lies are like viruses that spread and grow.

Be a mensch

When you think about the people you admire and want to emulate, what qualities stand out? For me, it's an openhearted attitude and a generosity of spirit. I like to think that nice guys—and women—do finish first. I realize that there are many people who have achieved success, at least temporarily, by being the most cutthroat ones in the room. They have wealth and grand titles, but their platforms are always a little bit shaky. The truly successful people are mensches. They care about others, and they're generous with their advice and support. It's a quality that I love in my husband. It comes naturally to Jono to think about what he can do for others. He always makes the time.

When I reflect about Jono's upbringing, I realize that he could have learned a different kind of lesson. As the son of the great financier Saul Steinberg, he was born to privilege and grew up with all the advantages money could buy. On the outside, it would seem that Jono lived a charmed life. But although he had material comfort, he also experienced firsthand the truth that money can't buy happiness. When Jono watched his father suffer the disastrous collapse of the empire he had built, and saw the way he was vilified in the press, he saw that the trappings of success are fleeting, and that the people who adore you on the way up are just as ready to condemn you on the way down. As a result, he has always tempered his ambitions with a sense of humanity.

Jono's family is extremely tight-knit, and he was especially close to his mother, who died a few months after we were married. Her death reinforced Jono's desire to pursue the things that really matter in life.

Jono has never been one for public displays. He is quiet and hardworking. I rely on him as a voice of decency. If ever I am troubled about making a tough decision, I know I can count on Jono to steer me in the right and ethical direction. Jono doesn't want to be known as the guy who made the most money. He wants to be known as the guy who helped the most people. It's no wonder I love him!

You don't have to cut someone else down to build yourself up. Sure, you want to do a good job and rise to the top in your profession, but that doesn't mean you have to kill the competition. Focus on your strengths. Build your own credentials. Make a case for yourself. I live by this principle.

Jack Welch told me, "One of the great things I've seen in people that are successful as leaders is that they have a gene of generosity. They love to see their people grow. They love to see their people get raises. They love to see them get promotions." That was certainly true of Jack. His generosity toward employees was legendary at our company. I asked Jack, "What if you don't have the monetary resources?"

"You've got recognition," he answered. "If you're starting a small company, you're all in it together. You can have pizza parties when you get a big order. You can have constant celebrations. Rewards don't have to be Mercedes or stock options or big deals. Constant recognition of the success of the team is a huge ingredient." Jack told me he learned this lesson when he was the captain of his high-school hockey team and while playing hockey in college. "I felt this enormous desire for the team to win, and to share the victories with everyone," he said. "Later, in business, it just came naturally to do the same thing."

These are simple lessons: do the right thing, reach

out, don't kill the competition, work for the team. But if you internalize them, you will be the most beloved and successful person in any room you enter.

Accept accountability

Everyone makes mistakes. You can't be successful without having a few failures along the way. By taking responsibility for your failures, you open the way to solving the problems. Maybe it's not a natural instinct to admit mistakes, but it's a great skill to practice. I've come to love doing it—to stand up and say, "That was me. I did it." It's liberating. Empowering. It eliminates the tremendous expenditure of energy it takes to pretend you're perfect, hide mistakes, or point a finger at others.

During the 2007 Valentine's Day ice storm and the Presidents Day weekend that followed, JetBlue Airways made a series of bad decisions that left thousands of passengers stranded, many trapped on the tarmac for up to ten hours. Some chief executives might have resorted to that threadbare excuse of "circumstances beyond our control," but not David Neeleman. He stood up and publicly apologized on my show, on the radio, on David Letterman's and the *Today* show, in full-page newspaper ads, and on the company's website. "We are sorry and embarrassed," Neeleman said. "You deserved better—a lot better—from us, and we let you down." His prompt action, his sincerity, and his promise to immediately remedy mistakes will go a long way toward building lasting loyalty.

The meltdown in the financial sector has demonstrated the importance of individual accountability. But in everyday life we don't have to wait for the integrity police to call us out. We are all capable of standing up while others run for cover.

Sleep at night

M any people are wondering how Bernard Madoff ever slept at night. How is it possible to live such a big lie, to knowingly defraud so many people, and to do it with a smile? Everyone loved and trusted Bernie. I've heard it said that sociopaths actually sleep very well because they lack the conscience to care about the damage they're doing to other people. We don't yet know if Madoff was a sociopath or just deluded. But when he finally told the truth, it wasn't because he had an attack of remorse. It was because the walls were closing in on him. A Ponzi scheme works only when money is coming in, but with the markets sinking, investors wanted to take money out and the scheme collapsed. You can't lie forever. Did Madoff know that, or was he arrogant enough to believe he would never get caught?

The impact of Madoff's actions on companies, charities, and ordinary citizens is beyond calculation. And there are more stories to come—the ripple effects of Madoff's fraud, the newly emerging mini-Madoffs in communities across America. I've been hearing for some time that more charges related to the scandal are pending, and that now appears to be the case. We also have a scandal unfolding in Great Britain with the financier Sir Allen Stanford, whose Stanford Financial Group has been charged with a scheme similar to Madoff's. And we all know there are many other instances we never hear about, of financial advisers either stealing from or mismanaging the money of their clients.

We look at these individuals, and we tell ourselves that they are different from us, that we would never allow our integrity to be compromised to that extent. But the road to hell is paved with small stones, laid one after another in the course of many years or a lifetime. I don't believe men like Madoff, as evil as they seem, started out with big plans to steal billions. Maybe they began by cutting corners here and there, and then they cut more corners to cover up their losses. Maybe they got so used to winning that they couldn't stand to be exposed. Maybe they became so comfortable with being feted, being rich, that they couldn't turn back. Lying became habitual.

Mort Zuckerman, whose charitable trust lost about $30 million in Madoff's scam, was at a loss to explain why Madoff didn't attempt a rescue when it became obvious the scheme was going to crash. "On one level, I cannot understand how he lost $50 billion," Mort told me. "I mean, I don't care if he was giving it away, it's not as if he wasn't able to invest the money and earn some interest on it." Likewise, Mort was baffled that Madoff didn't try to do something in the end to salvage some of his investors' money, even if it meant leveling with them that they should expect a hit. The fact that he just sat back and watched the scheme unravel without lifting a finger is, I believe, indicative that he just didn't care. Maybe he shed a tear or two as he was led away to jail to await sentencing, but it's doubtful that those tears were for the people he hurt. More likely, he was crying for himself and the prospect of life behind bars.

On June 29, 2009, U.S. District Judge Denny Chin sentenced Madoff to 150 years in prison, saying, "Here, the message must be sent that Mr. Madoff's crimes were extraordinarily evil and that this kind of irresponsible manipulation of the system is not merely a bloodless financial crime that takes place just on paper, but one instead that takes a staggering human toll."

People everywhere cheered the sentence, which was the maximum allowed by law. Unfortunately, no amount of jail time will make up for the money lost and the lives ruined by this scheme.

Bernie Madoff is responsible for his actions, but his path to prison was enabled by the blindness and greed of his investors and the fund managers who represented them. There was a giddiness about being allowed into Bernie's exclusive club. His investors viewed themselves as special. They were invited guests at a party that only the most privileged could attend. They ignored the tiny voices of doubt that told them there was no pot of gold at the end of the rainbow. Living in Bernie's stratosphere, where the air was thin, they were deprived of the oxygen of common sense and conscience. And so, when Bernie fell to earth, they fell along with him.

6

Adaptability

Stay open to change

In June 2009 I traveled to Russia for CNBC. My first stop was Moscow, where I was scheduled to broadcast *Closing Bell* live from Red Square and to interview President Dmitry Medvedev. Then I would go on to St. Petersburg, to participate in the St. Petersburg International Economic Forum.

On the flight over, I couldn't stop marveling at the fact that this trip would not have been possible only a few short years ago. I couldn't have imagined a global economic conference hosted by Russia, or that the Russian president would sit down with me for an open discussion about the future of the global economy. It was perhaps the greatest example in my personal experience of the powerful force of change—and the necessity of adaptability.

Russia is an interesting story of change and adaptability. When I was talking about the shift from communism to capitalism with one of my hosts in Russia, he recalled the days of communism on a practical level. He said, "One thing about Russia back then was when you needed something, whatever store you went in, it was always the same price. And there wasn't much diversity in colors or styles. As a man you either had a blue suit, a gray suit, or a black suit. But it was basically the same suit at the same price. One day I was shopping for a household item, and I saw it in one store near my house for three rubles and, of course, at another store miles away for the same three rubles. But then I went to London for college, and the same product was selling for the equivalent of five rubles there. And I thought, 'What crooks! I know that item is three rubles.' But actually it wasn't crooked at all. It was whatever the market would bear. Russia was a communist state and the U.K. was capitalist." It was an interesting take on the free-market society. He said that when the wall came down in Russia, the country wasn't ready for it. There was chaos because many savvy "thugs" came in and bought up everything at rock-bottom prices. By the time Putin came to power, Russia was desperate for some tough love and structure.

Every detail of our visit to Russia was planned in advance, and I even conducted pre-interviews in New York with embassy personnel. The people on both sides were nervous, an atmosphere that reminded me of being on a first date. Our two nations are not entirely comfortable with each other. We are both cautiously taking things one step at a time, conscious of our long, antagonistic history. As I stood in Red Square, televising *Closing Bell*, I felt a little chill, recalling the idea that was drilled into me when

I was a child: that Red Square was the center of an evil force. Those old notions are, to some extent, in our blood. We can't magically make them disappear. What we can do, though, is open our minds and embrace change, even when it is slow in coming.

For an American, Russia is a mesmerizing country. It is a place with very old foundations that is taking bold steps to modernize. The people are highly educated and skilled. You can feel it when you speak with them and have any kind of meaningful interaction. Russia is so focused on education—particularly math, science, and engineering—that it impresses you as being able to blow every other country away with its brainpower. So many geniuses grew up here—from scientists, to mathematicians, to dancers, to chess champs, to technology gurus like Sergey Brin of Google.

The question is, why do so many of them leave Russia? One reason might be the lack of economic opportunity. The Russian economy has been pummeled. The country faces a double punch: the credit crunch and the decline in the price of oil. Unemployment is high. Also, many people question the rule of law in Russia. They worry that the Russian government will change the rules in the middle of the game. As the story of investor Bill Browder shows, playing fast and loose with the rule of law will hurt foreign investment in Russia.

Bill Browder is CEO of Hermitage Capital Management, once the largest investor in Russia. He describes his experiences with the Russian government as "Kafkaesque."

In 2007, officials from the Ministry of the Interior raided Hermitage's offices, seizing documents, computers, and certificates that then enabled Russian officials to steal several companies. These companies were then used to forge documents and defraud the Russian people of $230 million in phony tax rebates. Browder told me he believed that such a massive fraud could not have occurred without support from the highest levels of the Russian government. To this day, there has been no official investigation. In fact, Browder was so frustrated in his attempts to get Russian media on the case that he launched a YouTube video telling his story and discouraging people from investing in Russia. Clearly, if Russia wants to become a land of opportunity, it will have to break the cycle of corruption that haunts its dealings with global businesses. And yet President Medvedev told me Russia is adapting to a changing global economy. He said he believes there is rule of law in Russia and is trying to encourage foreign investment in his country. Success in meeting this goal will take much flexibility in that economy. It will mean relying less on oil and gas and increasingly on other growth engines, such as technology, which will drive fundamental change throughout Russian industries. It will not be easy, but it appears the leadership of Russia recognizes the country must create a new mentality to survive in a changing, dynamic global economy.

Still, Russia offers great opportunity. It's rich in resources—minerals, diamonds, silver, emeralds—and is the world's largest producer of oil. I was eager to talk with President Medvedev about how his country was going to respond to the serious economic challenges it faced in 2009.

I met with President Medvedev at his lovely residence in Barvikha, a beautiful resort town a few miles outside Moscow. At forty-four, Medvedev is young and vigorous, popular with his people, and determined to advance Russia's fortunes and restore its position as a global power. Although many people believe he stands in the shadow of the prime minister, Vladimir Putin, Medvedev seems to understand that Russia is part of the global community and that the standards of the global community apply to all participants. And I think he feels a bit humbled by the economic shocks the Russian economy has experienced.

My crew and I arrived early, long before the president, to set up for the interview. We walked around to the back of the house, through grounds that were well kept and very secure, and entered from the back. The room where we were to conduct the interview was quite dark. The heavy wooden furniture and large fireplace gave it a somber, presidential aura.

For viewers, the setting would appear serene and quiet, but behind the scenes more than twenty people would be hard at work, including two cameras from CNBC, three from Russian television, two audio engineers, my producer, and several people from the offices of the Kremlin. Next door, two interpreters were setting up their operation. Although Medvedev speaks English, he was conducting our interview in Russian, through interpreters.

While I waited for the president to arrive, I sat down and began studying my notes. I was so engrossed that I was taken by surprise when Medvedev strode into the room, smiling warmly. He was charismatic and charming, but once he sat down for the interview, he was all business. We spoke for about forty-five minutes. The president was very candid about Russia's economic struggles. "I am not happy with the structure of the Russian economy," he said with a frankness that surprised me. "It's an obsolete, outdated structure, dependent on raw materials, which neglects innovation." But he remained optimistic, expressing confidence that his nation would be able to adapt. "Crisis is not only a dramatic event in our lives, but also a chance that destiny gave us, and we need to use this chance," he told me. "Crisis gives us a chance to change the structure of our economy."

After the interview, President Medvedev suggested we take a stroll around the grounds of his residence, and I happily agreed. The gardens were beautifully landscaped and lush, with a fountain as the centerpiece. I have to admit that it was a "pinch me" moment for me. I felt so proud and fortunate to have this opportunity. My mind was flooded with the amazing reality that the world was changing and that even the most resistant countries were adapting, out of necessity, to the demands of a new economic era.

In St. Petersburg, at the International Economic Forum, I shared the stage with President Medvedev; the former German chancellor, Gerhard Schroeder; the president of the Philippines, Gloria Macapagal Arroyo; Japan's prime minister, Junichiro Koizumi; and Columbia economics professor Robert Mundell. I also chaired a panel of some of the best business minds in the world, including Dieter Zetsche, the chairman of Daimler; Citigroup CEO Vikram Pandit; Elvira Nabiullina, Russia's minister of economic development; and Lloyd Davies, the former CEO of Standard Chartered and currently the U.K.'s minister of trade. The level of the discussion was impressive, and it was especially interesting to get their assessment on the subject of government's ownership role in business. The consensus from the panel and the audience was that government would have a significant stake in business for the foreseeable future. Whether that would be good or bad was almost beside the point since most of the panelists deemed it a necessity. Over and over during our discussion the assertion was made: "We have entered a new reality, and we have to adapt."

At night, when I finally made it to my room, tired but exhilarated by the discussions of the day, I was dazzled as I stared out my window into the bright St. Petersburg skies, experiencing the famed "white nights." In the warm season, there is daylight for twenty of twenty-four hours, and it never gets completely dark. The brightness of the midnight skies was something to behold.

Being in a historic city like St. Petersburg gives one a

sense of perspective. Before I left for home, I visited the State Hermitage Museum, which stands on the banks of the River Neva in the heart of the city. It is one of the oldest museums in the world, founded in 1764 by Catherine the Great. The museum boasts one of the world's largest collections of art and artifacts dating back to prehistory. It's an awesome experience to walk through the massive buildings and see the exhibits of art and jewelry. It wasn't just the beauty or the scale that impressed me, it was the commitment to culture and the creative spirit. Visiting the museum made me feel more hopeful for Russia's future, and it reinforced the feeling I had had repeatedly during my visit—that we are more alike than we are different.

As we start the second decade of this new century, the question we all face is whether or not we can adapt to the new challenges that face us—not just on a national or corporate scale, but individually as well.

Be Darwinian

Charles Darwin once wrote, "It is not the strongest of the species that survives, nor the most intelligent that survives. It is the one that is the most adaptable to change." This is the central thesis of Darwin's work, and it has relevance beyond the biological ability to adapt to the physical environment. For example, everyone in my business—the media business—is constantly being called upon to adapt to shifting circumstances and unexpected crises. Today we're facing a situation scarcely imaginable five years ago. The people who survive and grow will be those who can evolve. This truly is one of the laws of enduring success.

It's tough for people to be in a dinosaur industry, but it's the price we pay for human inventiveness. I know many people in the newspaper business, and it's been painful to watch the decline in recent years. News people really are in love with their industry. In the last year some of the great papers have disappeared, and Pulitzer Prize–winning journalists have been laid off. The shell shock is enormous. But it was also completely predictable.

It occurs to me, though, that we can get suckered by the new just as easily as we can get trapped in the old. Leading up to the year 2000 and coinciding with the turn of the century, there was at atmosphere of euphoria about the way technology was changing society. The tech boom was a bet on this new world, on our willingness to embrace change. It looked as if the bet was paying off. There was a giddiness among the dot-com billionaires. People were leaving their old jobs in droves to start Internet companies. They took wild chances, failing to see that the rapidity of growth was unsustainable. Their feet left the ground. The dot-com bust was a traumatic fall to earth.

The lesson of evolution is not just that change is necessary. The pace of change is also important, as the news business has shown. When newspapers began losing their audiences, their owners didn't just fold up the print editions and head for the Internet. The smart ones began a process of evolution—often painful and not always successful—involving a gradual introduction of online content. The organizations that ultimately succeed will be those that can develop the right formula over a period of years so they can effectively deliver content to a receptive audience. Slow and steady will win this race.

Personally, I am always looking for ways to educate myself about and engage in new technologies. The trick is to find those that enhance the delivery of news and information while bypassing those that don't. Remember, just because it's new doesn't mean it's automatically superior.

Avoid nostalgia paralysis

Marc Ecko is a wildly successful young entrepreneur. His clothing and lifestyle enterprises, headquartered in New York City, have redefined fashion and style for a new generation. Marc is frequently featured in the news for his offbeat, futuristic ideas, such as a big outdoor graffiti art exhibition in New York City, designed to celebrate freedom of expression, or his purchase of Barry Bonds's record-breaking 756th home-run ball for $752,467. In his typical egalitarian spirit, Marc started a website, asking visitors to vote on what he should do with the Bonds ball, and he received more than 10 million votes. The final verdict: send the ball to the Baseball Hall of Fame in Cooperstown, New York, with an asterisk (to signify that Bonds's performance may have been affected by steroids) affixed.

I enjoyed hearing Marc's ideas when he participated

in my televised series on innovation. One of his most useful was the concept of nostalgia paralysis. "From my own experience, you can't hold on to the past at the expense of the future," he said. "You know, this kind of head scratching, eye rolling, 'I've never seen that before' attitude. Success is a seductress, and when she shows up, she doesn't always dress the part. And you have to know not to discriminate against it just based on historical data or precedence."

Entire businesses can fall victim to nostalgia paralysis, as was the case with Kodak. When I interviewed Kodak CEO Antonio Perez, he talked about the difficulty of bringing his company into the digital age at a time when it was facing a terrible crisis. When he took the helm in 2003, Kodak was struggling to find its footing. Within the ranks there was some resistance to going digital. "We made our living creating and selling film," he said. "But when I went around the company and asked, 'How many of you have a digital camera in your household?' there were thirty percent of them in the beginning, then forty percent, then fifty percent, then sixty percent. So I told them: 'This is the deal. We either change, or we will cease to exist.'

"About one-third of the people were ready to go digital. Another third were absolutely convinced that expanding the benefits of film was the future of the company. Another third were in the middle. I worked with the people who were with me, who were ready to create a compelling vision." Antonio Perez didn't feel he had a choice about going digital. It was a question of survival. Eventually, those who resisted most strenuously had to make a choice about whether they would stay with the team. But Perez also knew that had the company not gone digital, there would be no team to stay with.

Recently, at a committee meeting at NYU, where I serve on the board of trustees, our chairman, Marty Lipton, made a very wise observation. Marty, who is seventy-eight and has had an illustrious career as a financial system innovator, warned us, "Don't fall in love with theories and fail to recognize that the winds are changing all around you." I realized that he was right. Learning to let go, even of one's most treasured ideas, is fundamental to succeeding through crisis. It can be very difficult to do, especially if you're a founder and the business is your "baby." But survival requires it.

I meet a lot of people who just want to relive the glory days. They're like former high-school football stars sitting around admiring their trophies. Nostalgia has a place. It's fun, and it feels good. Just don't get stuck there.

Know what you don't know

We all have holes in our knowledge base, and it's important to fill in those holes. For example, I didn't get a strong education in history because I was too focused on economics. But my husband is a big reader, and he loves to read biographies and stories about the founding fathers. Through conversations with him, and reading books that he has recommended, I have started to explore those areas and fill in the gaps in my knowledge.

I've noticed the same thing happening with my viewers. Before the financial crisis hit in 2008, the typical viewers of *Closing Bell* were well-heeled, financially savvy individuals with net incomes in the millions. Many were professional investors. But once the crisis hit, average people from all income levels and walks of life began to tune in. They were suddenly paying attention. They wanted to learn and understand, because they saw that their lives were being affected by what was happening in the markets.

One of the many things I admire about Oprah Winfrey is her devotion to learning and her passion for communicating what she has learned to her large audience. She's not embarrassed to admit that she doesn't have all the answers. When I went on her show, she didn't hesitate to ask the simplest questions: "What is a stock? What is the NASDAQ? What is the FICA?" She was willing to admit what she didn't know, and thus to begin a learning curve about investing.

"You know," she told me, "I grew up in an era when my father would say, 'Put your money in a shoe box.' When I first started making money, I was scared about diversifying beyond putting money in an insured savings account. I always wanted to say, 'Let me *see* my money. Show me the money!' I've gotten better. I'm learning."

I had a wonderful time on *Oprah,* simply enjoying being in the presence of someone who truly wanted to learn. The key to her success, I believe, is being able to put herself in the place of ordinary people and understand what they want and need to know. Every show is a teachable moment, and you come away thinking, "I learned something today."

The lesson, of course, is to never stop learning, no matter what industry you're in. It's so simple and basic, and it's what you expect of others. Would you want your doctor to stop learning after she finishes medical school? You would rightly expect that she keeps up-to-date about the latest medical developments so you receive the best possible care.

I have always been impressed by General Electric's commitment to training. GE spends over $1 billion a year on leadership training and education at its Leadership Development Center in Crotonville, New York. I've taken leadership classes there, and I've benefited from the tools they gave me.

One of my best models of excitement about learning is Jack Welch. Jack is seventy-three, and he is still in he process of being educated. "A thirst to learn is a key to success," Jack told me. "You've got to want to get smarter every day. I am thirsty to learn. Everywhere I go I want to know what they're doing, how they're doing it, why they're doing it. It's the most exciting thing in the world. When you're soaking up new information, you're also reinventing yourself. You're becoming more you."

Practice adapting

on't wait for a crisis to discover whether you have the ability to adapt. Life throws unexpected curves during the course of every day: The babysitter doesn't show up. The basement gets flooded in a storm. The boss puts an urgent project on your desk. There's an accident on the highway and you're late for an appointment. These mundane aggravations require adaptability— being able to shift course in an instant and make a new plan. If you work at handling the small stuff, you'll be more likely to cope when you get hit with the big curves.

Personally, I often find my best-laid plans for a given day unraveling before I've begun. It's the nature of my job. I've got to constantly shift course. But no matter what profession you're in, flexibility is required, and it's something you can learn. I think of my dad, running his restaurant. In his preparation, he would sometimes overpurchase food and then unexpectedly face a slow day without many customers. On other days he underpurchased, and there were too many customers. It was a constant balancing act, a learning process to work around the surprises. Likewise, I think of my mother juggling her dual roles of child raising and work. If one of us kids woke up with a sniffle, it was enough to throw off her carefully constructed routine, but she never seemed particularly rattled. Only later, when I was working myself, did I realize how difficult it must have been for Mom to handle so many responsibilities, and what a great mother she was to never let us see the pressure.

Find a hundred mentors

J ack Welch gave me sage advice about finding a mentor. First off, he surprised me by saying that "looking for a mentor is the dumbest idea in the world." Noticing my shock, he smiled and added, "What you want is a *hundred* mentors." Jack's point was that different people bring different qualities to the table, and if you hitch your wagon to one person, you're going to have a very narrow perspective. "Companies promote this mentor idea in a way that's not very smart," Jack said. "Any one mentor already has a history in the company. He has enemies. Maybe he's been a jerk at times. Why would you want to take on that baggage? By finding as many mentors as you can, you can assimilate the wisdom of different people. There are traits you can find in one person that are different from another person. Use them all."

Irene Rosenfeld, CEO of Kraft Foods, also had a helpful insight about finding mentors: look for them wherever you are—in or out of the office. "These relationships are often formed in funny places," she said. "One of my best mentoring relationships was developed at an off-site meeting with a Kraft senior executive when I was quite junior. We were doing one of those ridiculous team-building exercises where our blindfolded team had to untie a series of knots in a rope within a certain time limit.

For whatever reason, he decided that I showed tremendous leadership and creativity in this exercise and took me under his wing for the next few years. He remains a friend and trusted adviser to this day."

I like the idea of getting input from a variety of people. How do you begin applying it? I would start with making a chart of the areas where you need information, references, training, or other kinds of support. Then, as you meet new people, begin to fill in the chart. Your mentor chart, like your life, is a work in progress. You can keep it going through the years. One word of advice, though: Be sure to get beyond the stage of writing down names and actually ask for help. The first time you do it, you may feel butterflies in your stomach, but it gets easier as you find that most people really do want to help.

Be a sponge

There isn't a person alive who can't learn, who can't benefit from the wisdom and expertise of others. Successful people are like sponges, soaking up new information. Well, usually that's the case, but not always, as I saw during the 2009 World Economic Forum in Davos, Switzerland. During a fascinating session about harnessing new technologies. Russian prime minister Vladimir Putin shared the stage with Michael Dell. At one point Dell said to him, "Mr. Putin, we would like to do more in Russia. How can we help you?" Putin replied, "We don't need your help. We're not invalids. We don't have limited mental capacity." Michael Dell was shocked by his response, and he later said he felt as if Putin had taken his head off. It was a perplexing thing for Putin to say. Could Russia use more technological expertise? Of course! Strong people are not afraid to ask for help. In fact, most of the real movers I've met in business are like sponges, soaking up as much input as they can.

In 2009 I was invited to participate in the Aspen Ideas Festival, sponsored by the Aspen Institute, and to host *Closing Bell* from the site. The Aspen Institute is a think tank devoted to promoting ideas and solutions for the most pressing issues of the day, and the Ideas Festival has become its centerpiece. What an exhilarating experience to be among so many creative thinkers! Among the luminaries present were three former secretaries of state, Condoleezza Rice, Madeleine Albright, and James Baker; Supreme Court justice Stephen Breyer and former Supreme Court justice Sandra Day O'Connor; and many prominent people from business, science, and the arts. I had an opportunity to interview the Aspen Institute's CEO, Walter Isaacson, whose career is an example of a curious mind and a creative spirit. At fifty-seven, Walter has been the chairman and CEO of CNN and the managing editor of *Time* magazine. He is also an author whose remarkable work, *Einstein: His Life and Universe*, published in 2007, garnered many awards and much praise. Walter is clearly a man of ideas, with many eclectic interests. He believes that our future greatness rests on a fundamental civility—the ability of people with different views and experiences to come together and wrestle with the key problems of the day. I was inspired as I witnessed Walter and others at the Aspen Ideas Festival do just that. It's not that some of the sessions weren't lively and even confrontational. There were many heated discussions about the future of capitalism. But our discussions and disagreements occurred in the spirit of learning, enlightenment, and problem solving, not the kind of debate-for-debate's-sake we so often see in the media. At the Aspen Ideas Festival there was an acknowledgment that everyone's ideas have value, and that sharing, compromising, and adapting strengthens rather than undermines our potential.

After my experience at the festival, I thought about how great it would be if every person could participate in such a creative conference. I would strongly urge you to look around in your own community for similar opportunities—lectures, seminars, and gatherings that put you in the company of people whose ideas and experiences are different from yours. Always strive to find a new perspective, and don't be afraid to be challenged.

Embrace the world

Jim Rogers is the model of a global citizen. He has built an iconoclastic career as an investor, an author, a professor, and the creator of the Rogers International Commodities Index. In 2009 Jim published a book titled *A Gift to My Children: A Father's Lessons for Life and Investing.* The first rule, the anchor of his book, is

"You have to see the world up close if you're going to understand how it works." It's a simple message, yet one that he has put into daily practice. Jim is currently based in Singapore, and while some expats only hang out with other Americans, Jim immerses himself in the culture. While still living in New York, he and his wife, Paige, hired a Chinese nanny to make sure that their daughter, Happy, learned the language from a young age. They posted labels on everything in the house—the refrigerator, the table, the lamp, the bed, and so on—with its Mandarin name. Today, at ten years old, Happy is bilingual in English and Mandarin.

Jim's gift is his ability to completely transcend parochial biases. He recently told me, "The young Chinese are just like you and I were at twenty years old. They're working hard, and they don't see any limits on their future success." In effect, Jim has internalized the belief that all human beings have the same drive to achieve, even if their paths are different.

I had a great opportunity in March 2009 to report from the G-20 conference in London. You'd have to be pretty jaded not to be impressed with this event. The political leaders of the world got together and made the usual statement that they were willing to talk and work together. But this time it seemed different to me. There were conflicts, some of them serious. No big problems were solved during the week. But the overwhelming impression people had of this meeting was an appreciation that the world is pretty small after all. Even if major issues were not resolved, it was confidence building just to see the leaders of the largest industrialized nations strategizing together—with the United States speaking face-to-face with China, Russia, and others in a way that was not possible a short time ago.

It's easy to forget, but important to remember, that world leaders are human beings and personal relationships matter. Reaching out to others goes a long way toward healing differences. When you present a picture of unity and make an effort to speak their language, the possibility of true unity becomes real.

Plan your next ten jobs

A friend was whining about the lousy economy and said wistfully, "I can remember when people could expect to have a job for life." She resented not being able to stay with her company until she retired.

It was an amazing perspective, clearly out of touch with the way the world has been working for at least the past decade. It has been a very long time since people could count on having a job for life, much less *want* to stay in the same place for thirty or forty years. When you plan for your future, you shouldn't say, "What job am I going to have?" You should say, "What *ten* jobs am I going to have?" Chances are you'll wear many different hats during your lifetime. Why not anticipate?

When you're worried about your security, it's very hard to think clearly about how you'll shift gears when the time comes. But it's necessary. No matter what your position, take the time to consider how you can build and diversify your skill set. Examine your portfolio of knowledge, figure out where the holes are, and fill them in.

I tried my hand at several different jobs early in my career. When I started at CNN it was a young, scrappy company. Everyone was expected to wear many different hats. My experience there, working behind the camera—as a producer and writer and assignment editor—has allowed me to be the best I can be *on* camera because I understand the roles and agendas of the people around me.

Having a broad base of experience will allow you more security and greater opportunities. Look around you: Where can you get experience in another facet of your business? What skills can you learn that are recession-proof? How would your potential be enhanced if you were to learn and practice one new skill each year?

While you're making your list, open your mind. Don't limit yourself to the standard markers of professional experience. For example, when I first started broadcasting from the New York Stock Exchange, I felt a nagging sense of familiarity, as if I had been there before. I thought about it for a while, and finally the reason came to me. When I was in college, my mom got me a part-time job working at the OTB. Remembering that job, I smiled. In one sense, the OTB was a perfect training ground for the NYSE: a roomful of men placing bets in a highly charged environment. The NYSE had everything but the clouds of smoke.

The point is that our economy has changed and continues to change. It is vital to stretch yourself and obtain as many new skill sets as possible. Take a look at where the growth is in the coming decade. Former labor secretary Elaine Chao tells me we will need more than 1 million nurses in the coming years. The changing demographics of this country are causing this shortage. We are living longer and needing different things. Health care will be the growing area to watch, and it will attract a new surge of professionals to meet the demand.

When I visited Stanford University as a media fellow in 2009, I met with Laura Carstensen, the director of the Stanford Center on Longevity. Dr. Carstensen told me that the fact that people are living longer should not be viewed as a crisis. Rather, increased longevity should be considered an opportunity. Dr. Carstensen is committed to changing the negative concept of "retirement" and helping people be productive as they live longer by providing the tools they need to work and move around more easily.

Energy is another area that is hiring, particularly in areas related to alternatives to oil. Commodities and raw materials are in demand as populations grow in places like China and India. Increasingly, people are moving to cities, creating new issues: How do a growing number of people live close to one another and get around? These mega-trends will dictate where the jobs are and which skills will be needed.

Infrastructure is also an area to watch. We've seen an infusion from stimulus money, and as the global economy improves, we will see a tremendous investment in bridges,

roads, tunnels, and other essentials to keeping the infrastructure stable. At the same time, we will see a smaller
financial services industry and changes in the manufacturing sector, with the auto industry still under pressure. The
economy is changing, and in order to compete, it will be
vital to adapt to new leadership, new jobs, and different
growth. Mohamed El-Erian, of Pimco, the investment
management firm, calls it "the new normal." Take a look at
where the holes are in your own personal portfolio, and
think about what skill set you may need to thrive in this
new normal. Remember what Darwin said: *adapt*.

There are endless ways to stretch your experience
and build your résumé. In May 2009, during the height of
the recession, I learned of an interesting development at a
New York City volunteer organization called New York
Cares, a network of volunteers in operation for twenty-two
years. The executive director, Gary Bagley, told me that
the number of volunteers coming in the door had doubled
during 2009. People who had been laid off were not only
job hunting but also volunteering during their now-ample
free time. Altruism was one motivation. But what interested me was that many of these new volunteers were seeing it as a way to learn additional skills that would be
useful for their work lives. One volunteer, laid off from his
job in retail marketing, appeared on my Sunday show, *The
Wall Street Journal Report*, and said that his volunteer job
as a team leader and trainer at New York Cares added an
important dimension to his résumé. The idea of volunteering to improve one's marketable credentials, while at the

same time making a contribution, appeals to me. It isn't the usual method of résumé building, but it is absolutely valid. In addition to strengthening skills, volunteer work gives job candidates the extra benefit of showing potential employers that they are community-minded.

Hit the reset button

Mark Shapiro is a master of personal reinvention. Today he's the CEO of Six Flags theme parks, but for most of his career he was a programming whiz at ESPN. They used to call him the boy wonder because he was so adept at creating winning formulas for the network. Then, in 2005, another onetime boy wonder, Washington Redskins owner Dan Snyder, hired Mark to remake Six Flags, which was suffering from a tremendous debt burden.

What motivated Mark to make such a drastic career change? "I love sports," he told me, "but I had spent twelve years at ESPN. After negotiating the deals to bring *Monday Night Football* from ABC to ESPN and to bring NASCAR back to ESPN and extending our relationship with Major League Baseball for another seven years, I felt that the near-term future wasn't going to be as much about major growth as it was going to be about maintenance. When I looked at Six Flags, it was really the fix-it play, given all the debt we were inheriting and how the parks needed a lot of fixing. I'm not about maintenance; I'm about growth."

Mark has his work cut out for him, running amusement parks in a time when discretionary income has dried up. But he's not afraid of the challenge. "I don't believe families are just going to stay home and play in the backyard every single day of the summer. But where typically they might do three to five things together each summer, they're cutting it down to two or three. Competing for the consumer dollar is a bigger challenge in a much more crowded field. It's going to be about creating value that makes the difference between winners and losers."

The road to success at Six Flags has been rocky. Recently the company filed for Chapter 11, a necessary but painful process of housecleaning. Mark has stayed steady and optimistic throughout the process.

I love to hear stories of people who have the self-awareness, courage, and initiative to shift gears, and who are energized by a great challenge. One of my favorites is Joe Moglia. When I met Joe, he was the chairman of TD Ameritrade, but that wasn't his only incarnation. Joe's story is especially inspiring, given where he came from and how he has been able to reinvent himself time and again.

Joe grew up in Washington Heights, a neighborhood on the northern tip of Manhattan, when it was one of New York's toughest areas. His father was from Italy and owned a corner grocery store. His mother was from Ireland. Together they raised five kids in a two-bedroom, one-bath apartment. Their neighborhood was a place of lost dreams for many people. In fact, two of Joe's best friends didn't make it out of their teens. "One died of a drug overdose. The other was killed by police while robbing a liquor store," he told me. Joe was fortunate enough to get a scholarship to Fordham Prep, the Jesuit high school located on the Bronx campus of Fordham University. The school saved him. "Had I not gone to the Prep, there was a pretty reasonable chance I could've been with the guy who was robbing the liquor store," he said frankly.

Joe was a star athlete, and he had a good shot at going to college on a sports scholarship. Instead, his girlfriend became pregnant. He soon found himself married, driving a cab, and working for his father to support his new family and pay his tuition at Fordham University. The grind was relentless. "I really, really missed the involvement in sports," he said. He asked the Fordham Prep administrators if they would consider giving him a job as an assistant football coach. They did.

Joe found that he had more than one passion in life. As an economics major he came to love business, and he imagined himself becoming an investment banker on Wall Street. But he also loved coaching, and that's where he decided to plant his dreams. After sending out over one hundred applications, he got an offer from a private school in Delaware. In sixteen years, he coached five teams at five different schools, each time moving his growing family. In his last position, at Dartmouth College, Joe's team won two Ivy League championships. "I should have been ecstatic," he said, recalling the victories, "but I wasn't. I realized that if my passion for something I loved and was good at was starting to wane, then maybe there was something else I was supposed to do."

Joe's second incarnation, at age thirty-four, was a hard sell. He dusted off his old dream of working on Wall Street and began making the rounds. At the start, he gave himself three years to make it. If it didn't happen within that time frame, he'd go back to coaching. His approach was ballsy. Applying at firms, he'd tell them, "All I'm asking you to do is take a shot on me as a trainee. Frankly, it's not that tough a bet." He convinced them it would be worth their while to give him a shot.

Joe was accepted into Merrill Lynch's prestigious training program. He laughed, remembering: "There were twenty-six of us. Twenty-five MBAs and one football coach." Within three years of graduating from the program, Joe was Merrill's top producer. He rose through the ranks at Merrill becoming head of fixed income, then running the municipal division, and eventually moving to its private client division. Seventeen years after joining Merrill Lynch, Joe was named CEO of TD Ameritrade, one of the world's largest online discount brokerage firms.

Today Joe has found a way to engage in both of his loves—business and sports. In 2009, after stepping down as CEO of TD Ameritrade and becoming its chairman, he took an unpaid position as a career and leadership adviser to the University of Nebraska's athletic department. For Joe, it's the most gratifying thing in the world to pass on the lessons he's learned in sports and business to a new generation.

The point is, there is no limit to the number of times you can hit the reset button in your life. Once you realize that, there is a tremendous freedom.

I have the best job in the world. But I also have many other plans in mind. They may not come to fruition for ten or even twenty years, but I promise you that someday you'll see me teaching kids about finance. It's a passion I have, and when the time is right, I'll hit "reset" in some way. And maybe I'll develop a few other skills in areas I love, like running a business. One thing I know for sure: I am not done learning and adapting.

7

Humility

Hold on to your humanity

During the research for this book, my goal was to come up with the most important attributes of true success—and also to expose the trappings of success. Success, as has often been said, is fleeting. The challenge is not just to *become* successful but to hold on to your success. Throughout my interviews and interactions with people all over the world, I have heard repeatedly that the quality most responsible for a loss of success is hubris. We all know what it feels like and we all have seen it. But do we realize how damaging it truly is?

Hubris is about becoming too comfortable and believing that you are more special, more unique, and more important than others. Hubris is treating people poorly, and underestimating competitors and colleagues. People with hubris have their heads in the clouds, and eventually they stumble. Hubris is the opposite of humility. Or as Jack Welch once put it, "To get ahead, you have to possess self-confidence and humility at the same time. That combination is called maturity."

The management expert Jim Collins, whose book *Good to Great: Why Some Companies Make the Leap . . . and Others Don't* has been a phenomenal bestseller, pointed out that "the best CEOs in our research display . . . a remarkable humility about themselves, ascribing much of their own success to luck, discipline and preparation rather than personal genius."

I agree. Humility is one of the most important elements of success. I am fortunate to have met many people who seem to have it all but still manage to keep their feet on the ground—people like Bill Gates, Warren Buffett, and Jack Welch. Their success stories have one thing in common: a respect for their place in the world, an appreciation of where they came from, and an understanding that success can be attributed to many things, not the least of which is luck. Warren Buffett has often said that all of his talent and skill in making investments would have been meaningless had he not been born in the United States, where he had an opportunity to put it into practice. In his eyes the greatest secret to his success was the luck of his birth in the land of opportunity.

I have also seen examples of people who were brought down by a lack of humility. Bernie Madoff, whom I cited earlier for a failure of integrity, also suffered from arrogance—the belief that he was above law and morality. Integrity and humility walk hand in hand.

In my own life I am humbled by the realization that

my opportunity for success was built on the shoulders of my brave ancestors who sacrificed everything to make America their home. I think often of my grandfather, Carmine Bartiromo, sailing across the ocean on the *Rex* in 1919, and how much he left behind to create something new. I can't claim sole credit for my success. A big part of it is the legacy of my ancestors and the hard work and dedication of the teams I work with at CNBC.

Relax . . . you're human

Humility can be a hard quality for some people to grasp. We live in a culture where it isn't especially valued. We encourage people to present themselves forcefully, to brand themselves, market themselves, put a shine on their abilities, to never admit they made mistakes. We often confuse humility with a lack of self-confidence and view it as the antithesis of power. But humility is one of the most powerful weapons in business and culture.

Nobody likes to fail, but everyone does at some point. It's a fact of life. I struggled with this idea in the early years of being on camera. The business was so competitive, and I was front and center. I thought that I couldn't afford to make any mistakes, have a hair out of place, gain a single pound, make an incorrect analysis. In television, you're under a microscope, and you'd better be able to withstand the harshest scrutiny, or you're out. At least, that's the way it feels.

Since I was young and lacked full confidence in

myself, the idea of not being good at something was terrifying. I was often asked to speak in front of groups, and it wasn't something that came naturally. It didn't matter that I appeared on television in front of millions of viewers. Standing at a podium before a live audience was different. For a long time I was really terrible at public speaking. It was embarrassing. Fortunately, my boss at the time, Pamela Thomas-Graham, confronted me about my performance. She was blunt: "Maria, in your position people expect that you can stand at a microphone and deliver. But you get up there and you look like a deer in the headlights, clearly scared. You let down your audiences. You have to fix this."

It was hard to hear, a humbling moment. But I couldn't deny that it was true. So I took action and got a coach. It was an illuminating experience. Her first question was, "Tell me what you're trying to say—not the words you wrote down, but just conversationally. What's in your heart?" It changed my whole attitude about public speaking. Now I no longer write speeches. I jot down a few points and speak from the heart. And I'm no longer nervous or afraid, because my presentations are authentic, not scripted.

The lesson here is that success comes when you stop trying so hard to present yourself as someone you're not—when you relax and show your humanity. People respond to authenticity, even if you make mistakes or trip over a few words. They want to see a live human being, not a cardboard cutout.

Beware the tin ear

Before the taxpayers were asked to bail out AIG, Citigroup, Fannie Mae, Freddie Mac, and other financial industry titans, few people paid much attention to the personal excesses of the individuals at the helm. The standard justification was that the best and brightest deserved what they got, and pay and perks were rarely scrutinized. As long as the firms were making money for investors, who cared? But once the government got into the business of bailouts, people suddenly woke up. Maybe the fat bonuses and lavish perks that were customary for top executives were justified, and maybe they weren't. It is easy to understand why the public was so outraged as millions of people saw their savings and pensions evaporate. When the public observed the very people whom they deemed responsible for the mess riding high even as their own retirement accounts and savings disappeared, it seemed like a slap in the face.

A cautionary example of the tin ear is John Thain. I interviewed John many times over the years, and he is one of the best minds in business. As the chairman and CEO of Merrill Lynch, he showed courage and foresight at a critical moment and made the tough decision to salvage a dying company by selling it to Bank of America. John stayed on to manage the transition, and I fully expected that his skills would be put to good use in getting the company through the crisis. But twenty days after the merger, John was abruptly fired, sending shock waves through the industry. Three incidents preceded his firing. They may seem minor in the vast scheme of things, but to a country with no patience whatsoever for executive excess, they became John's undoing. The first was his decision to pay $4 billion in bonuses to Merrill Lynch executives on the eve of the merger, even though Merrill had lost $27 billion and the government was providing an infusion of TARP funds. The second was his request to directors that he personally deserved a bonus of $10 million for 2008 because he "saved Merrill" with the sale to Bank of America—a charge John denied later and that was never confirmed. The third was the revelation that he had spent over $1.2 million in the renovation of his office, including $131,000 for area rugs, a $68,000 antique credenza, a $35,000 commode, and a $1,400 wastebasket.

Less than a week after his ouster, I interviewed John in Davos, and he was looking humbled and a bit shell shocked. On the one hand, I felt for him. To have such a distinguished career shattered over "appearances" was an almost unthinkable blow. But I also felt the country deserved an answer about the excesses, and I asked him the questions everyone wanted answered. "John," I said, "Merrill paid out $4 billion in bonuses to Merrill top players. How can you justify losing $15 billion in a three-month period and still be paying out bonuses at a time when you were forced to sell to a larger player and you were going to the government for needed capital? How do you justify paying out all of that money?"

He gave the argument that "if you don't pay your best people, you will destroy your franchise." But I pressed him on this point, because it seemed to me that companies had to resize to deal with the new realities of the economy. John Thain was not alone in being blind to the public anger about bonuses, but he clearly had not been sensitive to the legitimate issue.

I also asked John about his expensive office renovation. This was just the type of thing that people jump on and salivate over—buying $1,400 wastebaskets while Rome burns. I wanted to understand how he could not see that this would be a public relations problem. "It was an environment where jobs were being cut and salaries were being cut," I said, "and the firm was reporting all of these losses. Did it occur to you at some point over the process to say, 'This is probably not the best judgment. I better put this off?'"

John was clearly embarrassed by the situation. "With twenty-twenty hindsight, it was a mistake," he said. "I'm sorry that I did that. And I intend to fully reimburse the company."

Unfortunately, John Thain came too late to the recognition that these actions had consequences. I think he'll come back from this. But it's an important lesson for people who aspire to reach the top rungs of business and industry: Humility in business is essential to success. And the greater your status, the greater the need for humility.

Laugh at yourself

I am often asked whether the nickname the "Money Honey" is offensive to me. My rhyming moniker was the creation of a reporter at the *New York Post,* and it just stuck. Well, it may be surprising, but I've never found it offensive. I don't take myself that seriously. I know that my viewers understand who I am and what they can expect from me. And nobody really calls me "honey"— except for my parents and my husband.

On some level, I suppose "Money Honey" is sexist, but it's also lighthearted. I don't think it has hurt me one bit. Maybe it has even helped humanize me.

There's a lot of silliness about me on the web, and I get a kick out of it. One of the most hilarious is the Maria Bartiromo Hairdex. This very clever guy devised a method of evaluating the stock market based on my cowlicks. When a friend directed me to the site, I had my biggest laugh of the day. It was so clever that I shared it with my friends and family. Sometimes they'll ask at the start of a market day, "How's your hair doing?"

When someone pokes fun at you and brings you down to earth, you have two choices: you can be annoyed, or you can enjoy the joke. When you have confidence in your abilities, you're free to laugh at yourself, and it's an endearing quality in successful people. In fact, humorous self-deprecation is part of our national culture, as I am reminded every year when I attend the White House Correspondents' Dinner. Since 1920 the White House and the reporters who cover it gather together to poke fun at one another, the president, and other top officials. The president's remarks are the most eagerly awaited. For a few minutes he becomes the stand-up-in-chief, and the country loves it. In 2009 newly elected President Obama brought the house down when he spoofed his supposed God complex. "I believe that my next one hundred days will be so successful, I will be able to complete them in seventy-two days," Obama said. "And on the seventy-third day, I'm going to rest." He also teased Vice President Joe Biden, Secretary of State Hillary Clinton, and congressional Republicans. In 2008, despite falling approval ratings, George Bush's sense of humor was on full display. He shared the podium with a dead-on impersonator who quipped, "How come I can't have dinner with the thirty-six percent of the people who like me?"

There's something comforting about a ritual whose intention is to bring the mighty down to earth. I've heard critics say that we should retire the dinner, that it's embarrassing to the dignity of the office. I disagree. When I think about the presidents who have served during my lifetime, those with the ability to be self-deprecating and humorous—Kennedy, Reagan, Bush—were far more successful than others. We want our leaders to know they're human.

Don't believe your own press releases

Too many people get caught up in a mentality where they start believing their own press releases. They get puffed up, thinking, "Yeah, I'm that good. I'm a freak of nature!" And when their world is upended, these people fall the hardest. On the other hand, those who maintain humility seem to rise above the crises.

Every successful person is endangered by hubris. Hubris is self-esteem without humility. I discussed this with Sir Martin Sorrell. Although he is incredibly successful as the founder and CEO of the WPP Group—not to mention being knighted by Queen Elizabeth in 2000—he is wary of hubris and thinks it can be a big problem for people at the top. "Hubris is fostered in the culture of many large companies, with the leaders getting surrounded by cadres of people who say yes to everything," he observed. "They have no one to help them keep their feet on the ground. And it's important to keep your feet on the ground. I know it's easy to say. We all have times when we let success go to our heads. But there are examples of great businesspeople who don't do that. I think Warren Buffett is one of those. I admire him for staying grounded. But one of the advantages of a financial crisis is that it shakes up people who have lost touch with reality. There's nothing like a kick in the backside to bring you back down to earth."

Some people have questioned whether President Obama also suffered from hubris. Early in his presidency he was riding high, but by the fall of 2009, with his approval ratings starting to drop, he took some actions that were questioned as presumptuous—such as traveling to Copenhagen to make a bid for Chicago to be home to the 2016 Olympics, expecting to woo the judges when those in the know were saying it couldn't be done; or his stubbornness about health care reform and an inability to see that people were divided on it; or his pushing government ownership of business. It began to seem as if Obama's confidence was inflated and a fall to earth was inevitable. I ran into one adviser who said, "The president doesn't listen to me or anyone else on the economy. He knows everything." Others made similar comments after being invited to the White House to discuss health care. "He brought all of us doctors together and said he wanted to hear our views," said one, "but instead read his own speech and left."

When I think of all the people I've met on my job, those who stand out and are truly memorable are those who remain down to earth. For example, Warren Buffett has been called the world's greatest investor. He is phenomenally successful. And yet, on a personal level, Warren truly is the "billionaire next door." He cares nothing for the perks and pretenses of the very wealthy. He has no interest in accumulating stuff. He lives in the same house in Omaha he bought in 1958, and he drives a modest car. He looks and talks like a regular guy. With Warren, what you see is what you get. He keeps it real. There are many other stories of humility in business.

This demeanor of humility is a critical quality for success. When I interviewed John Surma, the CEO of U.S. Steel, I expected him to reflect the grimness of a steel industry that is on the ropes. But I found instead a rare level of inspiration on the subject of personal success that should be a blueprint for others on how to behave when they reach the top. By any measure, John is a man of great achievement. He is also humble, balanced, and real. He has infused his struggling company with his own philosophy, and in fact he cautions other executives not to get, as his mother would say, "a swelled head."

"Just for the record," he told me, "I never think of myself as being all that successful. I'm just trying to do the best I can every day, and whatever's in front of me, I keep plugging away at it. But if I have any virtue, it might be that I try to have some balance in life, and I don't let the trappings of all this go to my head, which can happen easily. I try to keep a fairly level head about it. I don't get too excited when things are going really well, and I don't get too down about it when things aren't going so well."

Looking back on his immigrant grandparents gives John perspective on his own success. "I tell people that if my career had stopped eight jobs ago, I would have been happy. I had achieved a lot more than I expected. My grandparents were immigrants from Central Europe, and I'm way out ahead of my headlights. Every day I feel like I've gone beyond where I ever could have expected, and I'm glad to be here."

I was charmed by John's humility. He told me a story

about visiting his mother a few years ago at her senior apartment complex in suburban Pittsburgh. "I flew in from New York, where I had business, and I drove from the airport," he remembered. "It was about four-thirty in the afternoon, and my mother was in the common area with all her buddies, playing cards and chitchatting. And she looked at her watch and she said, 'Shouldn't you be at work?' So here I was, a CEO, and that's what she said. And I said, 'Nah, it's okay, Mom, I'm fine. I'm allowed to do this if I want. You don't really understand.' Well, on the way home, I thought, she exactly understood. She was saying, 'Don't get too big for your britches. You ought to be at work right now. You shouldn't be fooling around here.'"

One small, practical way that John stays grounded is through participating in a regular hockey game. The day I interviewed him, he told me, "This morning, at six A.M., I was on the ice at a hockey rink in suburban Pittsburgh, playing in a morning hockey league with a bunch of guys I've been playing with for a long time. And they don't care what I do for a living. I don't care what they do. We give each other a hard time. We play. We scuff a bit. Then I get a shower and go to the office."

I've always been attracted to people who can keep it real, and I watch for examples in the most ordinary circumstances. For example, I'd been impressed from afar with Jim McNerney, the CEO of Boeing. He's a smart executive, doing a good job. But I'd never met until we shared a table at an American Cancer Society dinner, and I saw for myself the wonderful personal qualities that I believe are the true secret to his success. Jim had his whole family at the table, including his brother, his two sisters, and his sister-in-law. Watching their interaction, I felt as if I were at an affectionate family gathering. Jim was so down-to-earth and filled with humor. I realized that no matter what happened in his life and career, I would always hold the impression of Jim as a good guy.

My friend Steve Van Zandt is a superstar. He is a brilliant performer who has been with Bruce Springsteen's E Street Band since the start. His role as Silvio Dante on *The Sopranos* brought him to new heights of celebrity. He has become incredibly successful, but he has never changed. He doesn't think of himself as a star. If you ask him, he'll tell you that he's just "little Steven from New Jersey." He keeps it real.

There are many stories of people who have reached the peak of success, but the ones you notice are those who never forget who they are.

Avoid the one-of-a-kind syndrome

No one is indispensable, but many leaders struggle with the one-of-a-kind syndrome: they think that if they step down, everything will collapse. This happens most frequently with people who start businesses that then become major enterprises. We've seen a recent example with Steve Jobs at Apple. When it became public that he was ill, it was presented as a tremendous crisis for the company. People were asking, "Can anyone run Apple if Steve Jobs isn't at the top?" I found the panic over-blown. Even though Steve Jobs is as innovative and unique as they come, the fact is that any leader is a temporary caretaker.

In 2007, when he was eighty-four, I interviewed Sumner Redstone, chairman and controlling shareholder of both Viacom and CBS, and I asked him, "What's your succession plan?" He had a surprising response. "Succession plans are for dead people." He then went on, "As John Malone [chairman of Liberty Media and then CEO of Discovery Holding Company] said to me when I met with him recently at a conference, 'Some of us are going to die, Sumner, but you're never going to die, so you don't have to have a succession plan.' That's my answer."

I thought he was kidding me, but he wasn't. When I pressed him and asked what his legacy would be, he repeated, a bit testily, "I'm not going to have a legacy. Legacies are for dead people. I already told you, I have no intention of leaving!"

I think Sumner Redstone really *does* plan to live forever. Later he sent me a bottle of MonaVie açai juice, which he promised was a magic elixir. But the practical reality is that the era of the imperial CEO is over, and we have seen some high-profile examples of poorly executed or nonexistent succession plans being the undoing of powerhouse executives and iconic companies.

Sandy Weill of Citigroup had a problem with succession. He was unwilling to allow his junior protégé, Jamie Dimon, to succeed him as CEO. In fact, he pushed him out and was later faced with the difficult dilemma of having a weak succession bench. When Weill himself was pushed out because of an investigation over conflicts of interest on Wall Street, he was forced to find a replacement fast. He chose Chuck Prince, his longtime lawyer, but Prince had never before managed an operation of such magnitude—hundreds of thousands of employees in almost two hundred countries. Prince had a tough time filling Sandy Weill's shoes. He was not liked by company underlings and apparently did not listen to his closest advisers. Citigroup's fortunes disintegrated in many ways under Prince's leadership.

Hank Greenberg also did not invest in a true successor at AIG. When he was forced to resign in 2005, there was no natural replacement ready to take over. AIG's new leadership struggled terribly until the government bailout in 2008. One source remarked to me, "Hank is a genius. The problem was he ran the company alone and had a strategy in his head. When he was gone, people did not know what to do."

Succession planning is one of the key jobs of the CEO and the board in any organization. A failure to have a succession plan can be indicative of insecurity, hubris, and poor leadership. When I spoke with John Surma, the CEO of U.S. Steel, he made an interesting observation. "If you're a successful person in a position of leadership, you can't let it become all about you," he told me. "The person who taught me that was John McGillicuddy, the CEO of Manufacturers Hanover, who died in early 2009. I went to his memorial service. John was a great guy, on our board for twenty years, and he was nice to me no matter what job I had over a long period of time. But I once heard him say that the leaders who get in trouble are the ones who forget that they're just there for a time, and they've got to do the right thing and then pass it along to someone else. For us, it's always about the company. I'm the thirteenth CEO of U.S. Steel, but I read all the time about what my predecessors did—J. P. Morgan, Frick, Carnegie, Judge Gary—because they fought many of the same battles I'm involved in. It's not that much different now. And if I can keep myself focused on what's important and get the company in a better position for the next person, whoever he or she may be, whenever he or she may arrive, then I've done my job. It's not about me; it's about the company."

Practice modesty

One of the most notable things about the Gates family—from Bill Sr. to Bill and Melinda—is their modesty. It is completely genuine, a product of who they are and the values they have held on to, even in the face of unimaginable wealth and success. I got an insight into this modesty when I interviewed Bill Gates Sr. I asked him if, when Bill was a little boy, he knew that his son was a great genius. He smiled at me and said, "Well, I think the answer to that is, basically, no." He went on to describe how each of his three children had special

MARIA BARTIROMO

qualities, and as parents he and his wife, Mary, tried to encourage their individual growth. In effect, Bill Sr. was saying that there were no "stars" in the family, and certainly no one was allowed to behave as if they were better than others.

Perhaps because of this grounding in modesty, the Gateses have managed to keep their feet on the ground and live reasonably normal lives. "There's no way there won't be some consequences to the fact that they are so rich, and they have such discretion about what they do," Bill Sr. acknowledged. "It's going to have some impact on the kids. And Bill and Melinda are very conscious of that, and they work very hard at conducting their own lives in a nonflagrant, nonextravagant way. So it's admirable. I really get a kick out of watching how carefully and how well they discipline themselves not to encourage extravagance, even though they are living very, very well. For one thing, they teach the kids that there are limitations, and they also teach them generosity and a spirit of caring for the world."

It's this same spirit Bill Gates learned at his father's knee. Clearly this is a family whose practice of modesty is a model for others. And the key, I believe, is that they don't just talk the talk, they live it too.

Be grateful

On some days I have to pinch myself. I've been reporting from the New York Stock Exchange for fifteen years, and I feel so grateful to have had this opportunity to broadcast my show and to work at one of the world's most important economic institutions. It's humbling and I cherish the opportunity.

Whenever I'm feeling self-doubt or worry, I stop and do a little exercise. I ask myself, "What are the ten things I'm most grateful for?" And I don't just think about them. I write them down in the notes section of my BlackBerry: I'm grateful for my husband, who loves me and makes me laugh every day; for my parents and siblings, who keep me grounded; for the people around me—my assistants and producers—who help me organize my life, understand me, and make me look good; for my great job; for my good health . . . the list goes on. My BlackBerry is full of gratitude! It puts my life back in perspective. I believe it's critical to my success, or to anyone's success, to cherish your opportunities and to be grateful for them.

No matter how important your job, it's important to have a sense of awe and gratitude. There was a moment between Barack and Michelle Obama, during one of the Inaugural balls, that I found to be so telling. Beyoncé was singing "At Last" as the new President and First Lady took the dance floor. Barack leaned in close to Michelle, and you could read his lips as he said to her, "How about this?" And she said, "Yeah, how about this." In that moment, they were just people, like you and me, feeling awe at their circumstances.

8

Endurance

Build your stamina

In the spring of 2009, while planning a one-hour CNBC special about Google, I stumbled across Paul Bond, who turned out to be one of the most amazing men I've ever met. Paul is the founder and owner of the Paul Bond Boot Company in Nogales, Arizona.

We were looking for a small business that had benefited from advertising on Google's AdWords search feature. We wanted a localized business, and my producer discovered Paul Bond Boot Company, which had been advertising on Google for a year and had seen sales jump.

At first I was reluctant to go to Nogales for the shoot. I was very busy with the "issues of the day," like the poor economy and the bank stress tests, and I didn't want the visit to interfere with what I thought was the big picture. But meeting ninety-three-year-old Paul Bond changed my attitude completely. I came away feeling lucky to have met this stalwart man, who loves his life and goes to work every single day with a spring in his step. What a rich life. What a story. I had to find out what made him tick.

When I arrived in Nogales, I was ushered into a huge, beautifully designed work space—the action center of the bootmaking enterprise. Paul Bond was strolling around in cowboy boots and hat, with the agility of a man half his age. He won me over with his style, and then he won me over even more with his substance.

Paul Bond has true cowboy credibility. His life story offers a compelling portrait of life in the American West. "I was raised on a ranch across the border from New Mexico," he told me. "I rode back and forth to school on horseback, and in high school I started working down at the saddle shop and the boot shop. My job was tooling spur straps and building boot heels." He laughed recalling his early days, especially his turn as a rodeo rider in the 1930s. "I used to ride the cavalry horses, and I loved to show off my stuff when they would buck. I got to where I could ride pretty good, and I created a trick riding act, and then I rode broncos and bulls for several years. But all the time I kept my interest in boot making. The rodeo riders were interested in a better-made boot, a handmade item, because most of the boots then were factory-made. So while I was riding in rodeos, I was also making boots." Paul made boots for some of the great names of the day, including Roy Rogers, as well as for the other riders on the circuit and the ranchers in the area.

After World War II, he got serious about the business. "It seemed like everybody had money after the war, and they wanted boots," he recalled. So he set up shop in the town of Nogales, and he's been there ever since.

I asked Paul, "How have you stayed so engaged and young?" Again, he laughed. "Well, I'm certainly not young anymore. But I am engaged. I enjoy making boots and staying involved with the customers. Our customers are very interesting people. They're adventurous, successful people that like to have something different and unusual. And the cowboys that wear our boots like to buy the toughest boot we can possibly make. So we delight in making the toughest cowboy boot that we can. It's so much fun." It's also a family affair, with his wife, Margaret, and son, George, fully involved. "It's just perfect for me," he said. "Each one does their own thing. My wife, Margaret, is a great designer. And George is great on the basics and on all this new type of advertising and communication. I would be totally lost in today's communication world without him."

I asked him the obvious question: to what did he attribute his longevity? "Interest in the business," he replied with a sparkle in his eye. "You know, waking up in the morning and being rarin' to go, to finish something I didn't finish the day before. Or having a new thought, and itching to get down here and take a look. Just the anticipation, the challenge of creating something."

He added, "It's all about having responsibility for something. I have always had some responsibility. I also have persistence. I love making things, and I love to persist and see them through. I see so many people who are successful, but they don't love what they do. They are unhappy. You have to love what you do to stay engaged. I am engaged. I love a lot of things, like playing golf, but mostly I love making boots, and I love getting up and coming to work every day."

It reminded me that the things we may often take for granted are actually the most important things in life: love what you do, work hard, be happy, be a good person, be engaged, get exercise. Paul Bond has led a full life, but he keeps coming back for more. I left the interview thinking, "That's the way I want to be. To live a very long life but die young."

Pace yourself

One question I'm frequently asked is whether you must be completely consumed by your work to be successful. People look around, and they notice that the most successful people don't seem to have much balance in their lives. They're always running at full speed. Young people trying to advance in their careers notice that the early birds and the late birds get the worms, and they strive to do both.

I discussed this with Jack Welch, because he was always a famous workaholic who said many times that balance was for the birds. "Balance is a bad word," he agreed, "but you may have misunderstood my point. It's not so much about balance as it is about setting priorities. For example, there wasn't an August during my career that I didn't take a vacation and play golf for thirty straight days. There wasn't a winter that I didn't take my kids skiing. Sometimes my job was my priority; sometimes my family was my priority. When I was working, I threw myself into it one hundred percent. When I was skiing with my kids, I threw myself into it one hundred percent."

I like the idea of being passionate about everything you do, in work and in play. Still, it's easy to overdo it. I admit that I am still trying to fix that tendency in myself, and I don't always succeed. Recently, I was feeling a little bit sorry for myself because my life was so crowded. I realized that I didn't have carefree days anymore. I remembered longingly those times earlier in my career when I'd get off work, call a friend, and say, "Let's go out for nachos." Where was that carefree Maria?

One night I arrived home from work so exhausted that I dumped my briefcase on the floor, fell onto the sofa, and announced to my alarmed husband, "That's it! I'm not working so hard anymore." Then I got a good night's sleep, and I was ready to go again the next morning. I don't know how not to work hard.

But what I've begun to realize is that doing too much is ultimately self-destructive. I tend to overbook myself, like an airline that sells more seats than it has. I told my assistant, "I'm turning over a new leaf. No more double booking."

She smiled. "Okay. And could you also agree to no more *triple* booking?"

The thing is, if you push yourself too hard, something

will suffer. Maybe it'll be your health, maybe your relationships. And maybe it will be your professional excellence. I learned that lesson in September 2008 after I
appeared on *Charlie Rose* to discuss the financial industry
meltdown. I did the interview at the end of a very long
day that was crammed with appointments. I didn't take
time to prepare, and it showed. I was awful. If I could pay
Charlie to burn that tape, I would.

The next morning, I was agonizing over my performance. "I am so disappointed in myself," I told Jono. "I
really blew it on *Charlie Rose*. I sounded stupid. I know
that material better than anyone else, but I didn't articulate it well at all."

Always the voice of calm and reason, Jono said, "Don't
beat yourself up. You took on too much. Something had to
give. You're not Superwoman."

When I interviewed Suzy Welch, she recalled the moment in her own professional life when she realized she
wasn't Superwoman. "I was a young working mother with
four children, and I was asked to give a speech to a conference of insurance executives in Hawaii," she said. "Thinking I had cracked the work/life balance, I took two of my
children with me. It was a complete and total disaster."

Suzy laughed, remembering the event. "As I was giving my speech to a roomful of executives, having ware-
housed my kids in a hula dancing class, my children burst
into the hall wearing hula skirts and ran up to the stage. At
that moment I knew that something had to change."

Suzy's moment of truth led her to reevaluate her

assumption that she could do it all. Clearly, everyone has a breaking point. In February 2009 Larry Summers, President Obama's chief economic adviser, took a lot of ribbing for dozing off at a White House summit on fiscal responsibility. And he was at the head table! I felt for him. Everyone needs their sleep.

Find your motivation

I f you can answer the simple question "What motivates you?" you can unlock the key to your own personal success. You have to dig deep. I'm not just talking about external motivations—acquiring wealth or position. Nor am I talking only about long-term goals. Long-term goals are important, but they won't necessarily get you out of bed in the morning. You have to find motivation in the moment. For me, it's the anticipation of finding out something new. I love preparing for interviews because it gives me carte blanche to call up whomever I want and get inside that person's head. I still get a charge out of listening and learning.

Motivation comes from having strong personal aspirations. That means that if you study hard and work hard, you can achieve anything. It's the American dream. We sometimes sell our kids short when we don't demonstrate the connection between hard work and success. A friend of mine told a story about an incident in a class at her son's high school. The instructor thought she was teaching them a lesson, but instead she was crushing motivation.

She had given them a test, and the students who studied, including my friend's son, did very well. Those who didn't study flunked the test. The teacher, disturbed by how many students flunked, announced that for the next test she was going to do a "redistribution of results." Everyone in class would get the grade of the lowest-scoring student. She told them, "You'd better all study hard so you don't drag the rest of the class down."

Predictably, though, some students studied and others didn't. She failed the whole class, and the lesson they learned was not the one she anticipated. The next time she gave a test, *nobody* studied. Why bother? If personal work and initiative didn't matter, there was no motivation.

When you're considering your personal motivation, you have to know there is a connection between what you do and what you achieve. Ask yourself what motivates you on a daily basis—what gets you out of bed in the morning? What motivates you on a yearly basis—learning a new skill or rising up a notch in the company? What motivates you on a long-term basis—where do you want to be in ten years?

Learn from your victories

The conventional wisdom is that you learn from your mistakes. But Garry Kasparov put a completely new spin on it for me. I asked him what he learned from his days playing chess. What was the lesson he took away from years of being the global champion? His reply was unexpected. He said, "Most people scrutinize their mistakes and say, 'I should have done this, I should have done that.' But I always scrutinized my victories and asked myself what I did right and what I could have done even better." Garry's method made a lot of sense to me. We can get stuck contemplating our failures, which say more about our frailties than they do about our potential. A positive perspective like Garry's can motivate us and focus our attention. I thought his insight was priceless, and it clearly came from the mind of a competitor. So scrutinize your victories and draw out the lessons to use in your next "match."

Deny stress its due

Sir Martin Sorrell once told me that in his mind stress does not exist if you're doing what you love and if you maintain your balance. For Martin that meant achieving balance between family, career, and society. "There are very few people who've managed to balance all three," he said, and he admitted that he didn't always get it right. Sometimes he sacrificed family or society during intense work periods. But when he saw himself slipping out of balance, he made a concerted effort to bring it back into his life.

The possibility that one could be successful without living in constant stress is very appealing—and productive, too. We all know that stress is a miserable state to be in, and that it can also kill. Stress can be like a bully, forcing you to ignore your own needs. It's appealing to think we can live without constant stress.

S. (Ram) Ramadorai has been on my show a few times, and he participated in my series *The Business of Innovation*. Ram is vice chairman of Tata Consultancy Services, a leader in information technology services. He is at the forefront of India's rise in technology, but he has acknowledged that we can't take anything for granted: these are unpredictable times. When I asked him how he remained steady during all the ups and downs, he replied, "The bedrock of my success has been keeping cool, having an open mind to new ideas and opinions, and having the patience to listen and learn at all times. In tough situations, it is all the more important to get different perspectives. Agility is another key trait that is required, which allows one to move from one problem to another and not get bogged down. Tough times allow one to do things that are not permitted during strong growth periods—to step back, reflect, and ask fundamental questions like 'Am I doing the right thing?'"

I like Ram's thoughts about agility and focus. In the current environment, it's easy to become scattered. There is so much information coming at us, and the market is moving so fast. The speed and chaos are manifested every day in the last hour of my show, *Closing Bell*, when the market is going crazy. You can get lost in the noise. Some people are even addicted to the noise. On *Closing Bell*, I have to think on my feet and respond instantly to events as they happen. But I'm always aware that I have to engage my brain before I open my mouth. If the market is going crazy, I can't go crazy too.

Joe Moglia, who has been both a sports coach and an investment banker, told me, "Both jobs are about how well you handle yourself under stress. Both jobs—coaching and banking—are about being able to put together a cohesive strategy that a team can execute against competitors. And both require an ability to get inside the hearts and minds of your people, having them pull together for a common cause."

Deepak Chopra has been a key figure in bringing Eastern philosophy to the West through his writing and teaching. With fifty books to his credit, his productivity as an author is astounding. Dr. Chopra told me that reducing the stress in your life and building endurance requires taking care of yourself in very specific ways, as I discovered when we had dinner one evening. I found his intensity and his focus amazing. When we were seated, he asked, "Would you like a glass of wine?" I said, "Yes, I guess I will." I noticed that he didn't order one for himself, and I asked him why. "I don't drink," he replied. "My observation is that alcohol keeps you up at night, and the most important thing in staying healthy is to get your proper sleep."

I stared at my glass of wine, and suddenly I didn't want it anymore. But Deepak only smiled. He is not the least bit judgmental or intimidating. He's merely an observer. And his observation, which he repeated to me several times in the course of the evening, was that sleep was the elixir of health and stability. "If you could do only one thing to improve your endurance," he said, "I would recommend getting eight hours of sleep every night." Dr. Laura Carstensen of the Stanford Longevity Center told me that while many people focus on keeping their bodies strong, job number one is protecting your mind. Cardiovascular activity, she points out, is critical to keeping your mind sharp; along with being engaged in work or something you love to do, it is critical to longevity.

Be the flight attendant on board

One evening at a dinner party, I was seated next to a man who runs the equities division of a major trading firm. Describing a typical day, he said, "I have to be the flight attendant." I laughed at the image, and asked him what he meant. He explained, "When there's turbulence on a plane and passengers start worrying that we are going to crash, I have to be the one smiling and making sure everyone is calm and no one is freaking out. I walk around the trading desk and I say, 'It's okay, this is why we get paid. Let's do it. Let's work.' And then I go into my office and close the door, and say, 'Oh, my God, I can't believe this is happening!' But I never show any anxiety in front of my team."

That's leadership. Maybe it's also a psychological advantage. If you speak calmly, you become calm. When I asked the historian Doris Kearns Goodwin why people turn again and again to Abraham Lincoln for insight, she replied, "Because of his emotional temperament and serenity in crisis."

When the financial crisis of 2008 first hit, the sense of panic fueled even more panic. It is difficult to explain the urgency, worry, and fear being felt that September and October. Every Friday for several weeks in a row, the heads of major financial companies met with government officials at the New York Federal Reserve. The question of survival was wide open. I remember waiting on Sunday nights for the release of news by government officials, timed before the Asian markets opened, and holding my breath wondering which giant would fall that week.

During that time, I appeared on the *Colbert Report,* a comedy spoof of the day's headlines. With his familiar brand of brutal irony, Stephen Colbert perfectly expressed the hysteria. "What the hell happened?" he asked me with bulging eyes. "Are there cannibals in the street? Zombie stockbrokers who've lost everything and rule the night? Should we invest in paper bags for people to breathe into until all of this is over?"

I laughed, in part because Stephen had so accurately captured the pervasive mood. But in those early days, the more dire the circumstances, the more I felt challenged to maintain calm. As I did my show on the floor of the Stock Exchange that day, with fury all around me, I tried to model the flight attendant standing steady in turbulent skies.

Stay disciplined

D iscipline is the cornerstone of endurance. It takes different forms, depending on what you do. For me, discipline means being prepared and knowing what's happening in the market and what questions I need to ask my guests. Another form of discipline is looking good for my daily appearance on TV. That means I can't stay up late or give in to the instant gratification of my favorite calorie-loaded pasta dishes. It will show up on my face and on my hips. When you're in a visual medium, you have to pay attention to personal appearance even when it's hard as hell, as is the case with the hosts of early-morning shows on my network. It takes an enormous amount of discipline to get out of bed at 3:00 in the morning and look good and be bright-eyed at 7:00 A.M. The viewers are in their pajamas, but the hosts can't be.

Discipline also means having short- and long-term plans in place, the idea behind Suzy Welch's 2009 book, *10-10-10: A Life-Transforming Idea*. "If you make reactive decisions, your life is living you; you're not living your life," she told me. Her technique is to approach every decision and situation with three questions: "How is this going to impact me in the next ten minutes? How is this going to impact me in the next ten months? How is this going to impact me in the next ten years?" Basically, 10-10-10 is a life management tool that Suzy initially devised during a period in her life when she had a number of difficult decisions to make. She felt that she was living too much in the moment, and that she needed a way to balance the short- and long-term considerations. She didn't want to always be flying by the seat of her pants, nor did she want to be so paralyzed by long-term consequences that she didn't act. In her book, Suzy tells the stories of many people who have increased their productivity and satisfaction using the 10-10-10 method. It really works. After I read *10-10-10*, I was surprised to find myself automatically reviewing the three tens when I had a decision to make or when I was preparing a story. I realized how easy it is for a reporter like me to live only in the moment. Everyone is in such a rush, so eager for the "scoop." I like the idea of working for more depth, of refusing to take shortcuts today that might compromise my credibility down the road. I try to keep the long view in mind as I plunge into the activity of each day.

Immerse yourself

One day I was sitting in my office, going over notes for my show, when I received a call from Francis Ford Coppola's office. "Mr. Coppola would like to meet with you when he's in New York next week," said the extremely polite and efficient secretary.

I wanted to blurt out, "Who, me?" I can still be starstruck. But I kept my cool and asked why.

"He's working on something, and he wants to discuss

it with you," she replied mysteriously. "He needs about four hours."

I was dying of curiosity. I explained that I couldn't do a four-hour meeting during the day, and she said fine and made a dinner date at Nobu, the fabulous Tribeca restaurant owned by Robert DeNiro.

I arrived at the restaurant right on time, and there was the man himself. I was dazzled and excited—this was fun for me. I really couldn't imagine what Francis Ford Coppola could possibly want to discuss with me. Normally I'm pretty tired by the evening, and if I have business dinners or events, I try to keep them short, but not this night. I was happy to give four hours of my life to one of the great directors of all time.

Francis was friendly and relaxed—a quality I would come to see as a key to his success. He got right to the point. "Maria," he said, "I am working on a movie project called *Megalopolis*. One of the characters is based on you, and I'd like to get to know you better and spend some time with you."

I confess I gaped. "This is kind of unbelievable," I said. I was completely won over.

He described the movie. The character, Wow Baltimore (what a name!), was a reporter broadcasting from the floor of the New York Stock Exchange. Wow came from humble roots and rose up through the ranks, just like me. Francis wanted to know me better so he could make Wow an authentic character. He grilled me about my

life story. Later he had dinner with my family and visited
the Stock Exchange as a guest on my show. I could feel his
keen observational eye taking in every detail.

Francis was consumed by the minutiae. It was an
exhaustive process, and I was very curious about it. I work
in the world of real business, so that level of research is
natural for me. But I figured that when you were producing fiction, it was a different story. It seemed to me
that Francis could have loosely based a character on me
and then gone on to invent a backstory, but his method
involves total immersion in each of his characters. His devotion to authenticity is what makes him such an effective
storyteller.

I was surprised to learn that Francis had been working on the concept for the movie for many years, and had
developed and rejected more than two hundred screen-
plays. I had rarely witnessed such attention to detail and
such perfectionism. This was a labor of love for him—the
opportunity to bring to the screen an epic portrait of New
York City. My character, and my contribution, was only a
tiny fragment of the whole, but he approached it as if it
were the centerpiece. As I spent time with Francis, I found
myself evaluating my own approach to projects. He inspired me to go deeper.

After he'd been studying my life for a while, Francis
arranged another meeting. "Maria," he said apologetically,
"now that I know you and have seen you work, I've come
to realize that Wow Baltimore is not like you at all."

"Oh." I'm sure my face fell.

He quickly added, "Wow Baltimore is evil." He went on to describe a conniving, cruelly ambitious woman who will stop at nothing to reach the top.

"You thought I was like that?" I asked, horrified. He assured me that he hadn't—that the character was actually a composite.

I appreciated Francis's honesty. He isn't a user, and he didn't want to risk my being embarrassed by anything he did. He even invited me to read for the part—as a kindness more than a serious offer. I am not an actress and have no intention of becoming one. A couple of gossip columnists had fun with it, though, writing, "Is Maria leaving Wall Street for the big screen?" No way. But it was a lot of fun reading for such a great director. Me!

Megalopolis is still on the drawing board, and it may never be made. Over the years, Francis has taken a lot of heat from critics who think he gets in the way of his own success by immersing himself in epic projects that are too expensive to make and too unwieldy to properly edit. But when I look at Francis I see a rare level of patience—the ability to listen and absorb information for as long as it takes. I suspect this trait grew out of his experience as a young boy when he contracted polio. He was confined to his bed, and he had to find ways of entertaining himself. He discovered that he could take his mind off his illness by becoming immersed in film. And that practice has made him a phenomenal craftsman. He is an amazing talent.

Work till you die

My uncle, Charles Managaracina, was a big role model for me. He was my mother's uncle, and he died in 2004 at the age of 104. I always believed that the secret to Uncle Charlie's longevity was that he never stopped working, even after he reached the century mark. He was in his garden pulling weeds until his final days. He had something to do, something to achieve, every day. And it kept him alive.

My professional Rolodex is filled with people well into their seventies, eighties, and beyond who have the passion and energy of young men and women. I love watching them. Sometimes I think that if you could get fifty eighty-year-olds in a room together, there's nothing you couldn't do.

In April 2009 former president George H. W. Bush invited me to participate as a panelist at an economic leadership forum he was hosting at his library at Texas A&M University. It was a good event, full of thought-provoking discussion. But I have to admit, what made the biggest impression on me was our visit to George and Barbara Bush's apartment before the forum. When we walked in the door, President Bush jumped out of his seat and hurried to greet us. At eighty-four, he was still full of vigor, physically and intellectually. When he turned eighty, the president made headlines by parachuting out of a plane, and he told me he planned a repeat performance for his eighty-fifth birthday. (It wasn't just talk. On June 12, 2009, the former president made a tandem jump with Sgt. First Class Mike Elliott of the Army's Golden Knights.)

Barbara came in, looking cheerful and full of good health. It was hard to believe that it was only five weeks after she'd had major heart surgery.

"Mrs. Bush," I said, "are you feeling better?" She chuckled, as if I were asking a silly question. "I'm fine," she said. "It was nothing. You know, they told me I could walk the dogs the day after surgery, and I did." Her sense of humor was still working perfectly.

Warren Buffett once said that he wanted his tombstone to read, "My God, he was old." Perhaps the secret to living fully is dying young, at an advanced age. A crucial element of enduring success is physical and mental strength. Protect it.

9

Purpose

Know what matters most

On April 22, 2009, I woke to the heartbreaking story that David Kellermann, the forty-one-year-old CFO of Freddie Mac, had committed suicide. As I went through my day, reporting from the NYSE, he was much on my mind—and, I found, on the minds of many people I spoke to. David's suicide brought us all up short. I had never met David, but by most accounts he was a very happy guy, with a beautiful family, doing work he loved. What happened to change that? We may never know the full answer, but clearly David was under enormous stress. In the months since the Treasury Department had seized Freddie Mac, he had been working long hours to restore the company in the face of billions of dollars in losses and government investigations. Friends reported that he had lost a lot of weight. Shortly before David's suicide, Freddie Mac's human resources chief asked him to take some time off, concerned that the pressure was taking a toll.

I can't speak for David Kellermann, but I have observed the dangerous spiral that occurs when people become lost in their jobs or in their status and can't handle the comedown. David Kellermann isn't the only suicide to mark these troubled financial times. There have been others. My heart goes out to them and their families.

Everywhere you go, you find that people are feeling beaten up. Some, like David Kellermann, just can't handle it. Others have taken the opportunity to look at their lives and reassess their purpose. They're saying, in effect, "Whoa! Wait a minute. What's important here?"

Finding and embracing the core purpose of your life will protect you during the upheavals. Your purpose is that which does not waver with hardship. It is not based on what you have, what others think of you, or whether you succeed or fail from day to day. Victor Frankl, the noted Holocaust survivor and author of *Man's Search for Meaning*, once described a person with purpose as one who "knows the 'why' for his existence, and will be able to bear almost any 'how.' "

Take a breather

I had just finished giving a talk to an audience of students at a southern university, and I was on my way to the airport. My driver was a young man, a senior who would soon be graduating. I struck up a conversation with him. He was telling me somewhat wistfully about all of the things he wanted to do. He wanted to travel. He wanted to study languages, do something interesting, get his nose off the grindstone. But it was all wishful thinking, because what he had to do was get started on his career. "It's pretty competitive out there," he said.

I found myself thinking about how young he was, about how fast time goes by. We all have those dreams of adventures we'd like to pursue someday, but how many of us ever get around to them? I thought about what Pepsico CEO Indra Nooyi had told the same students just an hour earlier. She said it's a nervous-making time to be looking for a job, but also an opportunity. An opportunity *not* to be focused on grabbing the highest salary or the top job, but to truly help others who may be worse off than yourself.

"It's a slow economy," I said, "so maybe instead of jumping into your career right now, you ought to take advantage of it by doing something different. Take the next twelve months to experience the world, get a taste of life, because you're never going to have this opportunity again. Once you get into the job market, there will be no going to Hawaii for a month, no backpacking around Europe. Now is the time. Or you could experiment with different job paths—things you've always wondered if you'd like. It might be the most important twelve months you'll ever spend. In the process, you might find out what you really love."

I'm sure he was surprised to be getting this advice from me, but I hope he took it to heart. So many students are scared silly about how they're going to make it after graduation. But they can't control the lousy economy; they can only control their own actions. And, once again, if you aren't committed to making a pile of cash the first year out of school, your options are wide open.

My nephew Jonathan graduated from college in 2009. "The race is on," he said. I smiled at his youthful urgency and told him, "I hope you stop and smell the roses." He laughed, but I was serious. "Sometimes I look back and I can't figure out what happened to the last twenty years," I said. "So, Jonathan, right now you have an opportunity to play the field, try a bunch of things, and figure out what you love. You don't want to look back after twenty or thirty years and wonder what happened."

Strive for fulfillment

People are crying out for meaning, whether they're at the top of the heap or struggling. They're aware of the need to be fulfilled, yet they worry that it isn't possible to have both fulfillment and success. For insight on this, I sought out the master, Dr. Deepak Chopra.

Deepak's insights were intriguing. He said that in his experience businesspeople really want to be the best human beings they can be—and to nurture the needs of others, not just themselves. Deepak said, "When we do our seminars at Kellogg School of Management, we say that if you're a leader, you have to think of all the people that you affect. If you really want to have a successful business, focus on your team. Make sure that your people are involved. Make sure that your employees are healthy, creative, and fulfilled, even in their personal lives. Don't make a distinction between personal life and business life."

I certainly agreed with him, in principle, but I voiced the concern I know many people have—that in the frantic pace of our world, economic well-being and fulfillment don't always seem to be compatible goals.

Deepak disagreed. "You have to consider the whole hierarchy of needs: survival, safety, material abundance, achievement, love and belonging, self-worth and self-esteem, higher guidance. You have to ask people, 'What do you want? Who are you? How can you make your lives more fulfilled?' And come up with creative ideas from the team in order to develop a vision, and then a practical way to actualize that vision.

"There's only one principle, by the way," Deepak said. "Pursue excellence and ignore success. If you focus on excellence, success will come." I found this statement to be quite meaningful and true. In my own career, I never set out to "be successful." I merely followed my dreams and decided what I wanted to accomplish. I had no idea where it would lead, but in my heart I know that I could call myself successful even if I weren't on TV every day, as long as I felt happy doing my job well and fulfilling my goals. Feeling content is true success.

Appreciate

Back in the late 1990s, when I was just hitting my stride at CNBC, I started to receive e-mails from a man calling himself Joey Ramone. He wrote very astutely about investments and the stock market, and commented about things I'd said on the air. For a while, I just ignored the e-mails. The only Joey Ramone I knew about was a punk rocker with a group called the Ramones, and I didn't think my e-mailer was the real Joey Ramone. I was pretty old-fashioned in my music tastes, with Frank Sinatra and Shirley Bassey on my iPod. (My husband always said, "Maria, you're the uncoolest person I know.") But one day, impressed by the intellect and knowledge expressed in the e-mails, I wrote back. And lo and behold, I learned that my e-mailer was indeed the real Joey Ramone, who happened to be very smart about money. We struck up an e-mail conversation and spoke on the phone several times. One day, after we had been communicating for a couple of years, Joey called me. "I wrote a song about you," he said. "Can you come down to CBGBs at midnight and hear me perform it?"

I laughed. "Joey, I'm flattered, but I have to be up at four in the morning. The only place I'll be at midnight is in my bed."

Joey was irresistible, and he convinced me to send a camera crew to film the performance. I was just blown away. Here was this long-haired rocker singing about me and the stock market. It was wild and touching all at the same time.

What's happening on Wall Street?
What's happening at the Stock Exchange?
I want to know
What's happening on Squawk Box?
What's happening with my stocks?
I want to know

I watch you on the TV every single day
Those eyes make everything okay
I watch her every day
I watch her every night
She's really outta sight

Maria Bartiromo, Maria Bartiromo, Maria
    Bartiromo.

He really rocked. But Joey never told me how sick he was, and I didn't know it would be one of his last performances. He died of lymphoma in 2001.

When I heard the news of his death, I felt an overwhelming sense of regret. I wish, just that once, I'd stayed up all night to see him perform. It taught me a lesson: Always take time to appreciate the unexpected gifts that come your way, because the people who send them may not be around tomorrow. Since that time I've been more attentive to the people around me, more eager to hear from my viewers, more appreciative of the insights that come across the transom from ordinary people.

Call your mother

We always talk about the importance of networking and establishing a base of support among colleagues and people in the business. But if you're lucky, you already have the most important support system there is: your family. So many people I've interviewed for this book told me that their family support system was the key to their success. These are the people who have your back, no matter what. A friend of mine laughingly related how his mother always told him he was a genius. "But she's my *mom*," he said. "Of course she thinks that." His eyes sparkled when he said it, though. Her unconditional support gave him an inner confidence that he couldn't get anywhere else, and he knew it. She also didn't hesitate to get in his business and offer her unvarnished opinion about everything.

I've always known that my family was my bedrock, so I have been lucky in that way—although I didn't always appreciate it when I was younger. I vividly remember an incident that occurred when I was a teenager. My boyfriend had broken up with me, and I was sitting in the basement crying when my mother found me. I spilled out my misery to her, and she comforted me as best she could. But I was really inconsolable and humiliated. I begged Mom not to tell another soul, and she said, "Don't worry, I won't." But then she went back upstairs, and seconds later I heard her telling the whole story to my father, sister, and brother. I was mortified. How could she? Today I look back on that incident and it makes me smile because it revealed a central truth about my family: we're all in it together, and we always have been. There's no such thing as *my* problem. It's *our* problem. That understanding has been essential to my success. I know I can succeed because they will be there to catch me if I stumble. Calling Mom and Dad, or my sister and brother, is like getting an infusion of strength and confidence. They're happy for me in good times, they back me up in bad times, and they always make me laugh.

Sir Martin Sorrell recounted a similar relationship he had with his father, who died in 1989. "I had an immensely close relationship with him," Martin said. "He was my best friend and my best adviser. I would talk to him—and this is no exaggeration—three or four times a day, even when we were in the midst of doing our so-called hostile takeovers of J. Walter Thompson in 1987 or Ogilvy in 1989, which were periods of intense activity. And I would talk to him as a friend, as a father, as an adviser, and as a counselor." I was touched by Martin's recollection, and I could imagine how much he must miss having his father in his life. Martin had the confidence to reach out and stretch himself in business partly because of the support of his family. Many executives have told me similar stories. Emotional support from family is so valuable to success.

No matter how busy you are, never be too busy to call your mother—or your father. Gaining strength from your family is the first rule of success.

Find what's important

In 1997 Gerald Levin was one of the most powerful media executives in the world. The CEO of Time Warner was widely regarded as a bold innovator and a classic workaholic who was on the job 24/7. But then his life took a tragic hit. Jerry's thirty-one-year-old son, Jonathan, a New York City public high-school teacher, was robbed and murdered by a former student and an accomplice.

Jerry dealt with the tragedy by pouring himself even more fully into his work. Looking back on that period, he admitted to me, "I'm the poster child for not paying attention to the most important thing in the world. The death of my son was probably the pivotal experience of my life. To not understand that, to not deal with it, to just return and work even harder—I hope people can understand and learn from that because I just put an iron curtain in front of my emotions. And our business culture actually encourages that. Your ability to negotiate and succeed comes not from being emotionally vulnerable; it comes from being almost a testosterone Superman. What a terrible failing on my part not to have taken that tragedy and tried to understand."

In the eyes of many, Jerry *was* a Superman. Three years after his son's death he made the biggest gamble of his career: the $106 billion merger with AOL. It was a catastrophic failure, and Jerry was forced out of the company. It was only then, with his career in shambles, that he woke up and realized what was important to him. Before that time, he told me, "all of my relationships—maybe even my relationship with myself—were based on Time Warner's destiny. If something didn't touch on any of the businesses of Time Warner, then I didn't have any interest."

Faced with unaccountable loss—first his son and then the work that gave him an identity—Jerry might have chosen any number of paths. He might have fought his way back to the top of business. Instead, he took a dramatic turn. He radically changed his life. He and his wife, onetime Hollywood agent Laurie Ann Levin, started Moonview Sanctuary in Santa Monica, California, an exclusive center dedicated to mental well-being.

At Moonview, Jerry tries to help other driven executives like himself find their inner core and pursue lives of meaning, regardless of their positions in business and society. Today, when he talks about how to be successful, he's definitely not the same man who ran a media empire a few years ago. Jerry told me, "My strong advice would be to find a calm, meditative state every day. With the tempo of executive life, that seems almost impossible, but it's probably the most important thing that you can do. I know I tried to find peace by just going into the screening room and watching a movie, or going to the Frick Museum and sitting in front of the little waterfall. It's just as important as preparing for an analyst meeting."

Ten years ago, Jerry might have scoffed at this advice, had it been given to him. It took a deep personal crisis to wake him up. He hopes that he can teach these lessons to driven executives before they have to learn the hard way, as he did.

Get your priorities straight

L ife throws curves that can change your priorities in a flash. That's just the way it is. I discovered that dramatically a few years ago when my mother got sick. I was on a hiking trip out West, and I called Mom to find out how her appointment with the orthopedist had gone. She was in the process of scheduling knee replacement surgery.

Mom was pretty agitated. "I don't know what the heck is with this doctor," she complained. "I want to get my knee replaced, and he said before we do the knee I have to go for a lung X-ray. So, fine—although I don't know what my lungs have to do with my knee. Now he wants me to have another one."

This didn't feel right. I got the doctor's number and called him. "Doc, what are you doing to my mother?" I asked in a teasing tone.

He was serious. "We found a spot on her lung," he said. "We have to check it out. Worst-case scenario, it could be lung cancer."

I couldn't believe it. "She never smoked in her life. She's healthy. She works out every day." But even as I said it, I was thinking about her years working in the smoke-filled rooms of OTB: secondhand smoke.

I immediately mobilized, calling every doctor I knew and setting up appointments. By the time I arrived home the next day, the diagnosis was in: stage-one lung cancer. Mom was scheduled for immediate surgery.

Suddenly, just like that, nothing else in my life mattered except my mother. Through her surgery and recovery, she never left my thoughts. At the time, I was very busy at work, running on several different treadmills. And it was as if someone had pulled the plug. Everything stopped. Mom was the priority.

She came through it successfully, and the cancer has never returned. Recently, she finally got around to having that knee replacement. But sometimes when I'm feeling overwhelmed by my work and think I can't spare a single moment, I remember that time—how in the urgency of the moment I was able to instantly shift priorities and do what needed to be done. And every time she complains about her knee, I remind Mom that her knee is our lucky knee. Without the knee tests and eventual CT scan of her lung, we would never have tripped over the lung cancer. Thank God for my mom's knee.

Don't forget to fall in love

Greg Waldorf, the CEO of eHarmony, the online matchmaking site, told me that when the economy was in free fall, his business prospered. Why? People were investing in love. "The economic downturn had the effect of shaking people up and forcing them to evaluate their priorities for the long term," he said.

As I thought it over, I recognized an important insight: The drive to succeed can be exhilarating, but it can also leave you flying without a net. It's the balance of love, family, and friendship that provides the cushion of a more balanced perspective. Many of the successful people I've interviewed have cited love as one quality they can't do without—even when they came late to the realization. Jack Welch has told me that meeting Suzy in his late sixties changed his life and opened his eyes to the gift of finding a soul mate.

Wake up laughing

When Jono and I got married, he told me a story that really touched me. He said, "Do you know when I knew I was going to marry you? It was the day you woke up laughing. And I asked you, 'Why are you laughing?' You said, 'I was dreaming about ice cream cones.' And I wanted to be with a person who dreamed so sweetly and innocently, and woke up laughing."

Happiness is infectious. We all want to be around people who are happy and who exude a positive, optimistic life force. Joe Plumeri, who is the CEO of the Willis Group, has been on my show a number of times. Joe is a great source when I want to know what's happening in the insurance business. I can say to him, "Just explain things to me as if I were your grandmother," and he's very good at that.

One day, in the midst of the crisis with AIG, I called Joe on his cell phone, and I got his voice message. And it was the happiest message I had ever heard: "Hi, it's Joe. Have a great day. Enjoy yourself." It made me smile. I felt better just hearing it. So I left this message: "Joe, it's Maria Bartiromo. I just want you to know that as soon as I hang up, I'm changing my voice mail message. Yours is so upbeat. I want mine to be, too. Call me back when you can. And have a great day."

That day, I changed my voice-mail message to "Hi, it's Maria Bartiromo. Thank you so much for calling. I am away from my phone. Leave me a message and I'll call you right back. Have a wonderful day. And don't forget to smile."

Create a legacy that lasts

Eli and Edythe Broad are quiet, self-effacing people who stay out of the limelight. In person, they give off a comfortable sense of being regular folks, in spite of their tremendous wealth and influence. Eli Broad is an interesting guy, a true rags-to-riches story. The son of Lithuanian immigrants, he built two major companies from scratch. But in 1999, after selling SunAmerica to AIG for $3 billion, he and Edythe decided to go into the business of giving back. And, they'll tell you, that's when the fun began. They created the Eli Broad Foundation and began looking for ways to use their money to make a difference. The foundation has been a major supporter of the arts, but their true passion is education.

"We looked at all the problems facing America and realized that if we are going to be a competitive nation, we need a far better educated populace than we have now," they told me. "The American K–12 public education has gone from number one in the world some thirty years ago to number nineteen. We thought, this is bad for the country and bad for our democracy, and what can we do to help?"

The Broads weren't interested in merely throwing money at the problem. Every one of their initiatives is practical and grounded in building long-term success. In particular, the Broads have focused on the management of urban school districts. Noting that superintendents are essentially CEOs of very large and complex companies, they felt that training was sorely lacking, and they created the Broad Superintendents Academy. The ten-month executive management program trains working CEOs and top execs with military, business, nonprofit, government, and education backgrounds to lead urban public-school systems.

The Broads also noticed that the best and brightest, those with MBAs and law degrees, were not going into the management of urban school districts. Eli told me, "We said, let's see if we can do for management what Teach for America has done for teaching." They established the Broad Residency in Urban Education, a two-year program that trains business and law school grads with several years of work experience and places them in managerial positions.

Today, while many philanthropic organizations are cutting back on their giving, the Broads continue to make large grants and to be involved in progressive education initiatives across the country. They say that this is the best time of their lives. They are clearly joyful to be creating such an important legacy.

But you don't have to wait for retirement to become philanthropic. I am equally impressed by those who have found that they can do well by doing good in the midst of their operating businesses. In 2008 I sat on a stage in Davos, Switzerland, at the World Economic Forum, interviewing three men who were sending out that message to a global audience: Bono, Michael Dell, and Bill Gates.

Bono is a rock star, but he has become known more for his vast charitable endeavors than for his performances. On this occasion, he was describing his newest venture, Project Red, a partnership with businesses to fight AIDS in Africa. Watching him sitting there, soft-spoken and wearing his trademark sunglasses, it was easy to forget what a huge superstar he was. "Celebrity is currency," he said, "and I want to use mine to do good." The two men beside Bono were superstars in their own right, and all three men were excited about cracking the code of business giving. The concept was basic: buy a Dell computer or a Microsoft software program, and a donation would be made to Project Red. "It's simple," Michael Dell said. "When you buy a computer, you can save lives."

"Innovation is our friend," Bill Gates added, "but it has to be innovation that thinks about the needs of the poorest two billion, not just the rich consumers."

Bono's genius lies in the powerful merging of consumption and giving. "It's all about connectivity," he said.

"A simple consumer act, buying a product, means—without spending any more money—that you are assuring that HIV AIDS is not a death sentence."

For Bono, and the men and women who partner with him, it isn't a matter of making a choice between capitalist principles and altruism. They are one and the same.

I found a similar sense of purpose in a group of powerful women. I was invited to a dinner called "an important dinner for women," hosted by Queen Rania of Jordan, Pepsico CEO Indra Nooyi, and Wendy Murdoch. They brought together three hundred prominent women to discuss maternal mortality around the world. Attendees included President Johnson-Sirleaf of Liberia, Barbra Streisand, Diane von Furstenberg, Christy Turlington, Martha Stewart, Tyra Banks, Tina Brown, Dorrit Moussaieff, the first lady of Iceland, and many others. Sarah Brown, wife of Prime Minister Gordon Brown of the U.K., gave an impassioned keynote speech to the assembled women.

What I especially loved about this dinner was experiencing the camaraderie that developed among the women, which generated a powerful joint determination to make a difference. The commitment was to get money and support to the women around the world who are facing maternal mortality because they don't have access to doctors to deliver their babies or because they lack basic resources, like clean water. The goal of the night was to have each of us do what we could to move the needle just a little. Wendy Murdoch said, "It's thrilling to have so many accomplished women behind the crusade to end maternal mortality." And one by one, many of us rose and made pledges to help, based on our own unique abilities and resources. I pledged to do stories on the grave challenges that so many women face. Diane von Furstenberg pledged to create a new design and donate a portion of sales to this special fund. It felt good to be involved in such an important goal.

Ask, "Am I happy?"

Deepak Chopra changed my attitude about seeking happiness as a road to success. "The number one trend in the world right now is well-being," he told me. "Whether it's the well-being of the individual, the well-being of the ecosystem, or the well-being of Wall Street."

Deepak described his work as a scientific adviser to the Gallup organization: he worked with them on creating happiness ratings in different parts of the world. "America came in way behind," he said. "It's number sixteen or seventeen out of about twenty-five countries. The happiest people in the world are in places like Nigeria, Mexico, Puerto Rico, and Bhutan."

"Why?" I asked. I couldn't believe it. But Deepak had a very simple explanation. "Because they measure happiness differently," he said. "Even Cuba was way ahead of the United States. I went to Cuba. I walked the streets and saw minstrels, lovers walking by the park, grandparents playing with their children. And I asked my government host, 'How come people are so happy here?' He said, 'Since we don't have any money to buy anything, we focus on relationships. We are a relationship society, not a consumer society.' And at that moment I suddenly had this insight: *Consumer*—what an ugly way to describe a human being who has insight, intuition, creativity, imagination. We are much more than just consumers, but we use such an ugly word to describe ourselves. We have the most money, but we are not the healthiest nation in the world. We have the best technology, and we're still not the healthiest nation in the world, nor are we the happiest. And we have the most weapons, and right now we're the most insecure. These are false gods. True fulfillment comes from inner peace and creativity and fulfillment and meaningful relationships."

I was moved by his words. Suddenly, it seemed so urgent to me that we learn how to be happy, and I asked Deepak how that lesson could be taught in America.

Again, his answer was simple. He told me that when he consults with corporate leaders, he asks them to sit down, close their eyes, and answer two questions: "Who are you? And what do you want?"

Their response is telling. "They never say, 'I'm the CEO of this multinational corporation and I want more money,' Deepak recounted. "They usually say, 'I'm a father. I'm a person whose word can be trusted. I want to make other people happy. I want peace and harmony and laughter and love.' So in the end everybody wants that, but they somehow have been misled to believe that if they make enough money, they'll get it."

Happiness can be consistent with work—in fact, it *should* be. As Warren Buffett told me, "I decided to start a company that made me happy. Why would I start a business that didn't make me happy?" Warren is clear that his success would be meaningless if he had to trade it for happiness. "I tap-dance to work every day," he said, "and when I get there it's tremendous fun."

10

Resilience

Get up and move on

Jono and I just celebrated our tenth wedding anniversary. We are very happily married, but the start of our relationship was so disastrous it almost never happened. I can say absolutely that walking down the aisle with Jono was one of the comebacks of my life.

We met in 1989. I had just graduated from NYU and was working at CNN. A friend invited me to a party being held at a loft in Greenwich Village, hosted by her friend's cousin. His best friend was Jono; their birthdays are a day apart, and they had a party to celebrate. Jono and I hit it off, and the next day he called me for a date. We arranged to meet at a restaurant in Manhattan at 7:30 P.M. The day of the date, I rushed home from work in Manhattan to Brooklyn, where I was living with my parents. By the time I got ready and was in the car, I was already half an hour late. Traffic was heavy, and as the time ticked away, I got more agitated. I'd really screwed up. I was going to be an hour late. I called the restaurant. "Is there a guy sitting at the bar, waiting?" I asked. The bartender handed the phone to Jono, and I blurted out my apologies. "Look," I said, "do you still want me to come? I'm stuck in traffic."

"Of course I want you to come," he said graciously. "I'll be right here when you arrive."

That was a relief, but even the most patient man can only take so much. When I finally arrived, the charming man I'd met at the party barely uttered a word. He was drained of enthusiasm. I sat through an uncomfortable dinner and thought he was pretty dull. When I got home that night, I told my mother, "That's it. This guy has no personality." Meanwhile, Jono was telling his friends how rude I was. He also said, "That's it."

A year went by. We didn't speak after that night. It was just one of those first dates that didn't go anywhere. One day I was working on a piece on small-cap stocks, and a colleague at work suggested, "Why don't you call Jono Steinberg. He has a magazine, *Individual Investor*, and he's the king of small caps."

So I called Jono, and we did the polite "long time no hear from" conversation, and then I asked him if I could come and interview him for the piece. He agreed, and we scheduled a time. At that stage I was working the overnight shift and trying to do everything I could to get ahead. The small-cap piece was something I was doing on my own. But the day after I scheduled an interview with Jono, I got a promotion and my job changed. I wasn't going to be doing the piece on small caps anymore. So I called Jono again. "I have good news and bad news," I said. "Which do you want first?"

"Give me the good news," he said resignedly.

"The good news is that I got promoted and I have a new job. I'm really excited. It starts tomorrow. So, the bad news is I have to cancel our interview, but we're still going ahead with this piece. I'm going to send my colleague Chris Huntington to interview you."

Jono was silent for a moment, and then he said, "Forget it. I'm not doing it." He was a bit peeved.

"Why not?" I didn't understand this guy one bit.

"I'm just not," he said.

I hung up the phone and thought, "What a jerk." Jono hung up the phone and thought, "What a flake."

That would have been the end of that, except Jono made a decision. In spite of everything, he liked me. I was amazed when he called me back two days later and invited me to go with him to a black-tie charity event in honor of his father, Saul Steinberg.

I figured, "What the heck?" So I dressed up and went with him. I was careful to be on time. And that night I fell in love with Jono. I saw the sweet way he interacted with his family members. I saw his decency. And I had fun. We became a couple and were married a few years later.

The fact that Jono and I are together is not a matter of luck. It all happened because we decided to take another look, not hampered by the rocky first impressions.

Resilience is the ability to bounce back, and it starts with having confidence that tomorrow can be better, even when there's blood on the streets today. Obviously, the only way you ever know for sure that you're resilient is when you're tested. But the qualities that allow for resilience can be cultivated.

I like to think that I have an optimistic gene—I'm sure that no matter what happens, I'll come back stronger than ever. I was raised in a family that held that belief.

Resilience is the opposite of being a victim. It means taking control of your own fate and participating in the outcome. Resilience is the ability to see possibility in the face of catastrophe, to say, "You know what? This setback is only a blip in the scheme of things. I'll learn something from it and go on."

A friend of mine who lost his job in the financial sector told me, "You know what the good news is? I'm thirty-nine. I'm going to make three more fortunes, and lose them, and make them again before I'm done."

Last summer I was playing golf at Lake Tahoe. My caddy had been a pro at the club, but due to job cutbacks he was now caddying to pay the bills. He was cheerfully philosophical about it. He told me, "You know, everything in life is temporary. One day you're a pro, the next day you're a caddy, and the next day you are a pro again." Great wisdom from the golf course!

The key to resilience is knowing that success is fleeting. It's easy to get so engulfed in your career, and to think it's so big, so enormous, that you can't survive without it. If you lose your job, it's traumatic, but that's temporary too. The good times may not last forever, but neither do the bad times.

Brace for impact

Few of us have dramatic moments like the one faced by the passengers in the plane that went down in the Hudson River. The pilot said, "Brace for impact," and seconds later they were in the water. No time to think it through or plan a course of action—just the splash. Clearly, the survival of the passengers depended on more than the pilot's skill. It depended on what they did next, once the plane was down. They couldn't sit in their seats and cry about what had happened. They couldn't wish for a different outcome. They had to act fast. I was particularly taken with the story of one woman who had a six-month-old baby. She was standing on the wing, clutching her baby as tightly as she could, and there was a raft in the water. A man in the raft held out his arms and called to her, "Throw your baby." She was frozen in terror. She didn't want to let go, couldn't imagine throwing her precious infant toward the water. But there was no time to wonder. She threw the baby to safety.

While it's true that crisis is a great motivator, you don't have to wait for crisis to find you. If your company is shutting down, you have to move. But you're a thousand times better off if you don't wait for the crash landing to take action. It's hard to make changes when times are good, but it's folly to leave your life to chance.

The mentality of waiting for crisis to happen before taking action pervades our culture. For example, we know that much of our country's infrastructure is crumbling. But it takes a bridge collapsing to really get our attention. Don't wait for your bridge to collapse, because by then it might be too late to get back up.

Keep standing

Jamie Dimon laughed when I told him that he seemed to be one of the few people who had emerged unscathed from the financial crisis. "I wouldn't say unscathed," he said. "I'd say battered and bruised, but still standing and fighting." I appreciated his honesty. It had been a rough period. But I was interested to know how in the midst of so much collapse, Jamie and JPMorgan Chase had come away so strong. Jamie has a reputation for being tough and unafraid to speak his mind. He is not your average buttoned-up executive. Jamie might be called a visionary, but he has always spoken about the dangers of big corporations, the arrogance that can ensue from power. His brutal common sense has been a key to his success. He also worked his way up the ladder, from being Sandy Weill's number two at Citigroup to running Bank One and eventually JPMorgan.

You can often tell a lot about successful people by looking at where they came from. Jamie's grandfather was a Greek immigrant from Turkey. He became a successful stockbroker and eventually brought Jamie's father into the business and taught him the ropes. Jamie learned business from the ground up, working in the family company while he was going to school. He's got all the attributes of a kid from the New York City borough of Queens who came from nothing, worked hard, and developed sharp elbows. And then when the going got tough during 2007 and 2008, he kept fighting, and along the way he did the right thing.

The experience of recovering from crisis creates inner fortitude. If you've survived one blow, you know you can survive the next one. As Jack Welch told me, "One of the things about being older is that you have been through it before. If you were running a corporation in 1981 or 1982, and I was, there was turmoil. The Japanese were going to take over the world, unemployment was 13 percent, inflation was double digits, we were going to lose, we were gone, we were done for. But we weren't done for. We've been through this before, and we will come back." The voice of experience is priceless in the comeback. If you do not have enough experience, when trouble hits be sure to surround yourself with those who do.

Jack also makes the point that resilience is about being able to make an honest assessment of yourself. He told me that he advises people who have lost their jobs to do a talent assessment. "Ask, 'Why did I lose this job? What did I learn from this experience that I can take somewhere else? What am I good at? What did I fail at? How can I translate this to another game?' Those are all very personal questions. But a massive self-assessment and a learning from change has got to take place. You can't sit home and suck your thumb. You can't be a victim, because a victim never wins."

Play to win every time

Few people exemplify resilience like Joe Torre. When he was the manager of the New York Yankees, he revived a struggling team and won four World Series titles. Now, as manager of the L.A. Dodgers, he has made that team a contender, winning the National League Western Division title two years running. In 2009 the Dodgers were only three games away from challenging the Yankees in the World Series when they were defeated by the Philadelphia Phillies. The Phillies went on to lose to New York in six games.

Two weeks after the Yankees claimed their twenty-seventh World Series title, I had a chance to sit down with Joe, who was in New York for the seventh annual gala for his charitable foundation, Joe Torre Safe at Home.

The last time I'd seen Joe was three years earlier when I'd been lucky enough to be invited to throw out the first pitch at a Yankees home game. Of course we talked baseball. I asked him how he'd felt to be so close to going to the World Series again.

"Success is a funny thing," he said. "We all want it, but once you have it, you have to repeat it. And that's where the pressure comes from. And these guys [the Yankees] were certainly up for the task. It is a fact that if you do something once, everybody will make a big fuss over it and you're proud of yourself, and it's something they can't take away from you. But the thing about it is you're validated by doing it again. You know the road, and it's bumpy, and you have to put up with a lot of stuff, and the media's a lot tougher now than when I started managing in 1996."

I asked Joe if he was watching the Yankees during the series, understanding them so well and thinking about what they should be doing. "You must have been inside their heads," I suggested.

"I know them," he agreed. "There was a lot of second-guessing going on about Andy Pettitte. Should he be pitching the sixth game on short rest? But knowing the kind of focused individual he is, I saw that he willed himself to win. It had nothing to do with physical well-being. It's a matter of just willing yourself to do something. I'm a firm believer in that."

I thought his statement was remarkable, and it could certainly apply in business, education, and every other arena. How do you will yourself to win? I asked Joe, as a manager, how he inspired that will in his players.

"Well, I have a young ball club now," he said, "and

I'm trying to find the right words to make it important for them." Coming from the more seasoned Yankees, Joe saw that they were able to achieve success time and again because "they weren't afraid of success." As for their 2009 victory, he said, "Once is never enough, four times is never enough, they wanted this bad. And I think the fans in New York certainly were ready for it." I could feel Joe's pride in his old team. At the same time I could see him calculating how to bring that winning spirit west and create championships for the Dodgers.

Joe has demonstrated resilience on a personal level as well. That's what his foundation is all about. Joe and his wife, Ali, founded Joe Torre Safe at Home in 2002 as a result of the impact that domestic violence had on him and his family. Growing up in Brooklyn as the youngest of five children, Joe used to stay away from home because he was fearful of his father, who regularly abused his mother. "Ours was an abusive household," Joe said, "and I was a very nervous kid. Even though I never got physically abused myself, I carried the scars with me even into my adult life. I was afraid of talking about it with anybody because I thought it was only going on in my house."

Many people thought Joe was incredibly brave to make his personal story public, breaking the silence that allows domestic abuse to occur. "It's something people don't want to talk about," he acknowledged, "so a lot of times they'll just close the door and say, 'Let's not even go there.' Also, when you mention domestic violence, it's always thought of as a women's issue, and I think a man speaking out about it gets a little bit more attention, and hopefully we can raise more awareness. When you raise awareness, people have to pay attention to it."

The Joe Torre Safe at Home Foundation has established Margaret's Place (named for his mother), a safe room in schools where young people can go and understand that they're not alone. "We try to give them coping skills," Joe said. "Obviously, they can't go home and say, 'Hey, Joe Torre says it's not right what you're doing.' But at least we can help them understand that they're not at fault. And they shouldn't feel guilty. We have great stories that have come out of very sad situations. We have a youngster that was going to join a street gang, and after three or four trips to Margaret's Place he decided to go to college. At Margaret's Place we always try to let kids know how important they are, because lack of self-esteem is a big part of why people repeat the abusive behavior they experienced at home."

In life as in sports, Joe Torre demonstrates that you can come back from the toughest defeats and make something of yourself. He has proved it personally, and through his foundation he is helping countless kids prove it for themselves. Being a champion doesn't mean winning every game. But it requires the will to want to win every time and the resilience to come back from defeat.

Prosper from failure

Recently I participated in a dinner discussion with professors and economists from Princeton and MIT hosted by Peter Thiel, founder and former head of PayPal. He is now a private equity investor and on the board of Facebook. Peter raised the question "How can you tell if someone or something will be successful?"

The consensus of the august group was that the most important predictor of future success is how a person handles failure. Although it may seem counterintuitive, I often hear the same philosophy from men and women who have achieved the most in their careers and companies. For example, when chairing a panel that included Lloyd Blankfein, the CEO of Goldman Sachs, I was surprised to find him so relaxed and lighthearted in the wake of the tumultuous 2008 Wall Street year. When I asked him why Goldman Sachs has been so successful, he replied with a smile, "Because we are so insecure." In effect he was saying, "Don't waste a crisis. Look it in the eye. Be on your toes." This attitude is the opposite of complacency.

Lee Iacocca told me that the signature event of his professional life was the near collapse of Chrysler in the early 1980s. He was never so energized and focused as he was during the period when he was figuring out ways to save the company. He took a lot of heat for his decision to ask the federal government for a loan, but he never thought of it as a bailout—just a short-term investment.

The day he paid back the government loan—three years early, with interest!—was the proudest day of his life.

I asked Lee, now eighty-four, how he felt about the 2009 bankruptcy of Chrysler, the company he fought so hard to save. "It's been painful for me to watch," he admitted. "I spent fourteen of the toughest, best, and most rewarding years of my life at Chrysler, fighting to save and then to build the company. Having said all that, I have to say that I'm still an optimist. The process of recovery is going to be gut-wrenching, but I am confident that the car companies will summon the best in themselves, as they have in the past, and come back stronger than ever. There are benefits to crisis, and one of them is that it creates a motivation for people to work together for success."

Looking at Lee, who seems as feisty as ever, it's clear that this isn't just false optimism. He has already seen the impossible once, when he brought Chrysler back from the brink. He believes a similar recovery is possible for the auto industry today.

Kathy Ireland, the former model who now runs a women's clothing and lifestyle brand that sells over $1 billion in products a year, told me, "Rejection served me very well." She explained that she had grown so used to it that it didn't daunt her. She knew how to move through it. "I failed so many times before starting my business. My modeling background caused people to not take my ideas seriously as a CEO," she said. "But I didn't listen. And what I would say to women who are trying to get into business is to turn down the noise of rejection."

Patience, perspective, calm, and confidence are the qualities of survivors. But foremost in every comeback story is the ability to see that no crisis lasts forever. For me, doing *Closing Bell* at the Stock Exchange is a metaphor for that. During the peak trading hours, the Stock Exchange is a noisy, messy place. I'll never forget September and October of 2008, when there was so much wild trading. Paper was flying, people were dashing around, the numbers on the board were plummeting. But at 4:00 P.M., the closing bell sounded and it just stopped, as if someone had pulled a switch. The floor became quiet. By 4:30, it was nearly empty and the maintenance workers were silently pushing brooms. By 5:00, the lights were dimmer and the floor was clean. It was almost peaceful. As I walked across the floor on my way out of the building, I marveled at how the scene of such wild disarray could have so quickly grown still. That transformation stands as a reminder to me that in the face of great chaos, the calm is just ahead. It keeps me centered.

Fight on

You've got to hand it to Hank Greenberg: nothing stops him. Most people would have just thrown in the towel after experiencing the five years Hank recently went through. First, as I noted earlier, in 2005 Eliot Spitzer, then the attorney general of New York State, publicly accused Hank of fraudulent business practices. In the wake of the accusations, the AIG board forced Hank to resign as chairman and CEO of the company he had built. By the time criminal charges were dropped, the damage had been done; the public's mind was made up. Then, in 2008, Hank had to watch AIG's collapse, a result of bad business decisions that were made after he left the company.

What does Hank have to say about it? "It's not over yet," he told me with absolute conviction when we spoke in the spring of 2009. He is still pushing, still trying to resolve the tangled problems of his industry and the government ownership of AIG coinciding with the great loss in value of AIG.

Hank doesn't waste much time reliving the way he was wronged. "It's painful, in the sense that such accusations hurt your dignity," he said. "On the other hand, I'm pretty thick-skinned."

What motivates Hank these days is no longer a desire to get his reputation back. He figures that the people who know him and have done business with him over a lifetime already know he did nothing wrong. Rather, he is determined to correct the gross missteps that occurred at AIG after he was forced out of power. He believes that had he been running the operation, it would not have failed. "The people they put in to run the company knew nothing about running a global organization," he said. "They were massacring the company instead. What happened to AIG should never have happened. I am fighting for the thousands of employees who lost their life savings and pension funds, who lost hundreds of millions of dollars. I'm fighting for all of them because I believe that they've been wronged."

I admire Hank's spirit. A lot of eighty-four-year-olds in his position would have just taken their toys and gone home. Not Hank. "I'll fight until there's no hope left," he told me with great emotion. "I won't give up until I've done everything that I humanly can do. I'm a fighter. That's just me. I can't be different."

Don't waste energy on outrage

When a friend of mine lost her job with the collapse of Lehman Brothers, I called her on her cell phone. "I heard the news," I said, "and I'm so sorry. I just wanted you to know I was thinking of you and I wish you the best."

She replied, "Maria, I am sitting in the Hamptons right now having a glass of wine, crying. But you know what? I'll get through it."

What she didn't express was anger or resentment. She didn't complain about what a bum deal she got. She wasn't outraged. That was a relief, because there seems to be a frenzy of outrage in the air these days. Everyone is mad as hell and not going to take it anymore. But when I think about how our economy is going to make a comeback, and how those who suffered losses are going to be restored, I'm pretty sure that the driving force won't be outrage. Outrage may feel good, and it may even jump-start action, but it won't solve any problems. Mostly, it's just an ineffective distraction.

The public has been legitimately outraged by some instances of a lack of integrity in the banking industry, especially the payment of huge bonuses to some of the people responsible for the trouble. Congress fixated on the bonuses because the politicians could smell blood in the water. But eventually it became clear that outrage was dictating agendas, and that wasn't healthy. Congress was operating on adrenaline and emotion, instead of putting emotion aside and deciding what was really important. It's much easier to stand on a soapbox than it is to do the hard work of figuring out how the country is going to get back on its feet.

I asked then New York Attorney General Andrew Cuomo, who had been investigating the payout of bonuses by financial firms receiving government help, "Do you worry that politicians and the media have been fanning the flames of class warfare? The bonuses outrage and 'business is bad' theory seem to be obscuring other per-haps more important issues, like fixing the financial sys-tem and getting credit moving again."

"That is a fair point," he said. "People are rightfully upset about Wall Street abuses and excess. And we need to address those issues. But we also need to be very care-ful and not let that anger become counterproductive and a distraction. I also think Wall Street should be taking a long hard look at the philosophy of incentive compensation. I don't think bonuses are always bad. The question for Wall Street is, can it design incentives that promote the long-term health of the firms, as opposed to just hitting short-term numbers?"

The first step to recovery is learning to trust again in a system that has been badly broken. As Andrew put it, "People don't go back into the water until they see that the shark is dead." Andrew understands the psychology of public anger. I agree with him that trust must be restored. But the process doesn't occur when you're busy breaking windows. It requires thought and care and time. Colin Powell, whose steady demeanor is one of the keys to his success, has often said, and practices, that you first "get mad, and then get over it."

On a smaller scale, we all have periods in our lives when we're tempted to operate on anger, resentment, and fear. It's human nature. There's a brief comfort in feeling bad, but the key to success is to step away from the raw emotion. Russell Simmons, a quiet, thoughtful guy who brought hip-hop to the mainstream as a way of giving a voice to an unheard community, told me that his motivation was to transform attitudes. He sees hip-hop as a form of poetry and says, "Those who look inside are less fearful and angry."

Earn a comeback

I first met Mike Milken twelve years ago. My husband knew him through his father's business, and Mike invited us to his home at Lake Tahoe where the Milken Family Foundation was having a retreat for medical experts dedicated to finding a cure for prostate cancer. I was impressed by the way Mike brought together these fiercely competitive experts with outsized egos and got them to collaborate on developing joint directions in cancer research. It was a remarkable event.

Since that time I've come to know Mike very well, and I've participated in the Milken Institute Global Conference on several occasions. His think tank has shifted the dialogue about the economy in positive directions, tackling health care and education in particular. And Mike's philanthropic efforts, particularly in the arena of health, have been truly impressive.

At sixty-three years old, Mike Milken is an example of a man who has redeemed himself through good works—in effect, earning a comeback.

In 1990 Mike was convicted of securities fraud, sentenced to ten years in prison, and ordered to pay $200 million in fines. At his sentencing, he broke down in tears, apologizing to those he had hurt. But words of apology, sincere or not, are not enough to pave the way for a comeback. Only deeds can do that. It didn't seem possible that he would ever recover his reputation or his standing. And yet in a short time he has done more for cancer research than most people.

Mike Milken ended up serving only twenty-two months of his sentence. The month he was released from prison, he was diagnosed with advanced prostate cancer, which had spread to his lymph nodes. His comeback was built on this personal crisis. He devoted himself to medical research, contributing so much energy and money through his foundations that *Fortune* magazine called him "the man who changed medicine."

Many influential people have stated that Mike merits a presidential pardon, although he has yet to receive one. (Both Bill Clinton and George W. Bush declined to issue pardons, despite intense lobbying on his behalf.) That's not to say that Mike's failures will be forgotten, but he has written a new chapter in his life. It has been a long journey, and it is still continuing.

John Chambers, the chairman and CEO of Cisco Systems, has a comeback story that is very different from Mike Milken's. But the structure of his comeback is similar: great success, followed by a huge fall, followed by a steady climb back up a long hill.

At the peak of the dot-com boom, John was considered one of the brightest stars in technology. He was universally applauded as Cisco's stock soared to $80 a share. Then the bubble burst, and Cisco's stock plummeted to $14 a share. Things got so rough for John that he had to hire bodyguards.

When we talked about that period, John said, "The worst thing for me during the dot-com bust was that people questioned my integrity." I could see the pain it still caused him, many years after the fact. Motivated by the desire to do the right thing for his company and to prove his integrity, John engineered a long climb back. Today the company is thriving, and John's reputation is one of a strong, global-minded leader with integrity.

Milken and Chambers, and others like them, earned their comebacks by digging in their heels and working tirelessly to turn bad situations into good. Their failures— be they moral, intellectual, or strategic—were not the defining story of their lives.

Write your epitaph every day

A mentor of mine once said, "You have to think about what's going to be written on your tombstone." I was quite young at the time, and the idea of my tombstone seemed very far away. But I appreciated the point. How do you want to be remembered? What mark are you going to make on the world? I think about Bill Gates. After all he has done to lead the computer revolution, likely he'll be remembered more for giving away $100 billion to cure disease than for his role as a captain of industry. He may not have planned it that way, but his life took a different course than the one he expected as a young man.

The question of legacy has sobering implications in these times when we're witnessing people who were amazingly successful for their entire careers suddenly hitting bottom. Will people remember their remarkable achievements or their bitter struggles? Will they be deemed successes or failures?

It gives you pause. You can't always control the way you are judged by others. Nothing is guaranteed. But you can live your life in a way that makes you content and happy. That is true success.

Acknowledgments

One of the biggest lessons I've learned about success is that you can't achieve it alone. I have never met a truly successful individual who does not rely on the enduring support of colleagues, friends, family, and others who have helped pave the way.

For me, writing this book has been a demonstration of the value of collaboration. I am deeply thankful for the contributions of many people: all of my colleagues at CNBC who every day speak to investors and leaders around the globe, tapping into their success and empowering all of us; Catherine Whitney, my cowriter, for her dedication, and for making this process seem so seamless; Wayne Kabak, for being so engaged in this project; John Mahaney, for his leadership at Crown; Bob Dilenschneider, Joan Avagliano, Christina Ciocca, and Ken Sunshine; Jesse Derris, Anne Finn, and their teams.

Thanks to everyone at the New York Stock Exchange where I broadcast most days. It's been the best seat in the house for fifteen years. In particular, thanks to Dick Grasso, Rich Adamonis, Duncan Neiderauer, and so many others— and all of my friends on the floor.

I am also thankful every day for those who have supported my career and encouraged my aspirations: Jack Welch, for his leadership and friendship; Jeff Immelt, for his knowledge and encouragement; Bob Wright, for his vision; Jeff Zucker and Mark Hoffman, for allowing me to do what I love to do. Thanks, Mark, for leading CNBC to greatness! Thanks also to Jeremy Pink, Tom Clendenin, Brian Steel, Susan Krakower, and everyone at cnbc.com, and CNBC in Europe, Asia, and the Mideast and Africa; to the teams at the New York Stock Exchange and Investor Media; thanks, Han-Ting Wang, Alex Crippen, Joel Franklin, and Katie Kramer, for always making it look so easy.

To Lulu Chiang, for making it happen, and for your sheer talent and dedication; Deborah Nikiper and Michael Harwood, for your support, and for adapting to constant change. Thanks, Margie Martin, for your talent and hard work. Thank you, Rosario DaSilva. Special thanks to Ciro Scotti for your collaboration.

I deeply appreciate the participation of the many successful people I had the great fortune to interview, who shared their tips and secrets to success. And I am thankful to my family, the foundation of my success, and to my extended family. Last but not least, thank you, Jono, for everything.

Index

About the Author

MARIA BARTIROMO is the anchor of CNBC's *Closing Bell with Maria Bartiromo* and host and managing editor of the nationally syndicated (to more than two hundred stations) *Wall Street Journal Report with Maria Bartiromo*, rated as the most-watched financial news program. Earlier in her career she was a producer, writer, and editor for *CNN Business News*. A graduate of New York University and now on its board of trustees, Maria Bartiromo lives in New York City with her husband, Jonathan Steinberg.

Printed in the United States
by Baker & Taylor Publisher Services